THE STORY OF JOSEPH

Imam W. Deen Mohammed®

ISBN- 9781500761790

CONTENTS

__Imam W. Deen Mohammed__, leader of the largest community of Muslims in the United States of America passed on September 9, 2008. We pray that his work continues to grow and serve humanity as he would have desired it to, through all of us who have benefited so greatly from his teachings. Ameen

Structure, Guard And Publish The Knowledge

"We need knowledge, then we need protection for it. How do you protect knowledge? Some people say, "You protect knowledge by not letting anybody interfere with it. Don't let anybody change it. Publish it! When you publish it, people know it. That's its protection." Yes! If you want to protect your knowledge, publish it! When you publish it, it is protected and the people know it. But if you keep it locked up to yourself, you will die and your knowledge will die with you. Or your enemy will get a hold to it and he will publish it after you in a corrupt form.

Thus, Allah (swt) says. "And We have revealed it for the express purpose that it should be propagated." Yes! That is its guarantee that it will be protected. When it's propagated in its right form, then the people will inherit it directly. They don't have to listen to what you have to say. You won't have to tell them what Prophet Muhammad (pbuh) said, they got it directly. It was published by him in his lifetime.

If we want to guard the knowledge that we have, we must publish it. The more people know about it, the more it is guaranteed that it will live and it won't be changed. The less people know about it, the better the chance that it will die with us, or be changed. Yes! We structure the knowledge and we propagate the knowledge." ***Imam W. Deen Mohammed***

Abbreviations Clarified

G-d for G-d
In this book the word G-d is written as G-d for the respect of the word "G-d" because some people mirror to disrespect it with the word "dog".

SWT for Subhana Wa Tallah
The abbreviation after Allah (SWT) means "Subhana Wa Tallah" in Arabic which means "The Sacred and The Mighty" in English.

PBUH for Peace Be Upon Him
The abbreviation after Prophet Muhammad (PBUH) means "May the Peace and Blessings of Allah (G-d) be upon him" in English and "Sal Allahu Allahi Wa Salam" in Arabic.

AS for Alayhi Salam
The abbreviation (AS) means "Alayhi Salam" in Arabic, which means "May Allah (G-d) bless him" in English.

THE STORY OF JOSEPH

For the benefit of our guests, for those who are perhaps visiting for your first time The Muslim greeting As-Salaamu-Alaikum, it means peace be unto you. And we open with the standard prayer; the title of this prayer is Al-Fatihah in Arabic. It means the opening. And I will read the translation of the opening prayer of the Muslims given by one Asian scholar in the translation of the Qur'an. He gives the English translation as, "With G-d's Name, Most Gracious, Most Merciful. Praise be to G-d. The Cherisher and Sustainer of the worlds. Most Gracious, Most Merciful. Master of the Day of Judgment. Thee do we worship and thine aid we seek. Show us the straight way, the way of those on whom thou has bestowed Thy grace. Those whose portion is not wrath and who go not astray. Ameen.

G-d, Most High says in the last revelation, the last of the revealed books, the Qur'an, revealed to Muhammad, the messenger, peace and blessings be on him—in the chapter by the title or by the name Joseph, in Arabic or the Qur'anic language Yusuf. In the Arabic or Qur'anic language, G-d says, Laqad kana fee Yusufa wa ifwatihi ayatul-lis-sa-elin. In the translation given here by the same translator, the Asian, Pakistani translator, it reads in english, "Verily in Joseph and his brethren are signs". And then he has in brackets, "or symbols". And he continues, "for seekers". And then he has in brackets, "after truth". So it reads, "Verily in Joseph and his brethren are signs or symbols for seekers after truth".

Now let's quickly note or recall some of the major developments or incidents in the life of Joseph or Yusuf, the Qur'anic term. He was one of twelve brothers. He felt close to his youngest brother, to the younger of the brothers—whose name is given in the Bible as Benjamin. Here in the next verse of this same chapter titled Joseph, the English translation is given, "Truly Joseph and his brother are loved more by our father then we, but we are a goodly body. Really, our father is obviously wandering in his mind".

So, here the brothers are talking among themselves about Joseph and Joseph's brother Benjamin. And it seems that they are jealous of the affection that the father has for Joseph and Benjamin. So they begin to plot. And the

Qur'anic words are given here –that they said, "Slay you Joseph or cast him out to some unknown land. That so the favor of your father may be given to you alone. And there will be enough time for you to be righteous after that."
So, here obviously, they are planning an unrighteous thing. And they are saying, "Let's get rid of Joseph first and then think about being righteous. We will have enough time after we get this problem out of the way to be righteous". The one sensitive one, one who was conscious among them, he said, "Slay not Joseph. But if you must do something, throw him down to the bottom of the well. He will be picked up by some caravan of travelers."

They said, "O our father, why does thou not trust us with Joseph, seeing we are indeed his sincere well wishers". Now, here they are trying to establish themselves before their father as brothers who care for the well being of Joseph and wish him nothing but good.

The Father, his name is Jacob; in the Qur'anic language Yacub. They said, "Send him with us tomorrow to enjoy himself and to play, and we shall take every care for him".

Jacob said, "Really, it saddens me that you should take him away. I fear that a wolf will devour him while you attend not to him." Well it seems that the old man didn't trust the brothers. He felt that Joseph might get caught by the wolf while Joseph is with them. They said, "If the wolf was to devour him while we are so large a party..." Now, how large were they?—10 brothers. "While we are so large a party –then should we indeed first have perished ourselves." So they are really sounding very convincing. Saying, "We would perish ourselves before we let anything happen to Joseph".

So, they did take him away and they all agreed to throw him down to the bottom of the well. The Arabic or Qur'anic term for bottom is ghayaba—and this word ghayaba is an allusion to a situation wherein there is no light, no guidance, and no hint as to how to escape or to get out of that situation. This is G-d speaking now, "And we put into his heart the message of assuredly—thou should one day tell them the truth of this their affair—while they know you not".

So, it seems that they were not themselves aware of Joseph—his importance, his true identity. G-d inspired Joseph, even while he was in that situation, that one day, he will, himself, bring to their mind the true case that they had involved themselves in or had brought upon themselves. Then they came to their father in the early part of the night weeping. They said, "O our father, we went racing with one another and left Joseph with our things and the wolf devoured him. But thou will never believe us even though we tell the truth." They stained his shirt with false blood. He said—that is, Jacob, the father, "Nay, but your minds have made up a tale that may pass with you. For me, patience is most fitting against that which you assert. It is G-d alone whose help can be sought."

"Then there came a caravan of travelers. They sent their water carrier for water, and he let down his bucket into the well. He said, "ah there –Good news! Here is a fine young man. So they concealed him as a treasure, but G-d knows well all that they do. The brethren sold him for miserable price—for a few dirhams counted out. In such a low estimation did they hold him." Now here we get something else about their relationship with Joseph. They regarded him as being of not much importance. They didn't see him as a valuable being, valuable person. They held him in low esteem. They estimated him to be of very cheap worth, of small value. But he must have been a big problem. Here is something of small worth but a big problem, because they went to all of that trouble to get rid of him. So, he was of little value to them, but a big problem.

It is important to understand the shirt. They took his shirt and they stained it with animal blood, wolf blood, or animal blood—to make the father think that he had been eaten or taken by an animal. Now don't forget the verse that we read from the very beginning which says, "And surely, or indeed in Joseph and in his brethren is a sign for the seekers after truth."

A Caucasian, European-American writer, he wrote a book about our trials and suffering during slavery and after. And he titled the book,"The people who walk in darkness." He took the title from a Bible saying, "The people who walk in darkness have seen a great light." I understood after reading this small book on our misery that he was saying that the great light that we had seen was freedom; that the light of freedom was guiding us and directing us and influencing our actions and that we would not stop until we had freedom. That is what I understood from his book that in spite of all of the suffering, terror tactics of the Klan to put fear in us, and to frighten us away from freedom. In spite of the lynching, all of the bad things that we suffered, we continued to seek freedom. We didn't give up. We continued our search for true freedom.

So, he said, "The people who walked in darkness have seen a great light." And now we see Joseph was put in the bottom of the well—in a situation that was dark –that didn't allow any light for him. Then he was sold into slavery-put in darkness, and a lie was made against him by his brothers. His brothers tried to make his father believe that he had been taken by an animal. There is a lot I want to say. There is a lot that I am not going to say. I am going to let you make your own conclusions. At least in some of these areas here—some of the report on Joseph, I will leave it for you to make your own conclusion.

Now let us look again at their moral make up. They said, "Let us do this to Joseph and after that, we will have time to be righteous." Well, here is a people who are putting aside moral obligations. They are postponing moral obligations to get something done, that they want to have done. Now, a man in Egypt bought him. The man in Egypt bought him and he said to his wife, "Make his stay among us honorable."

Akrime is the same word used when G-d said "And We made honorable every son of Adam." So if G-d made honorable every son of Adam, then Joseph was already honorable, but he had been put into a situation that denied him or deprived him of his honor. He was in a situation because of the conniving and the conspiracy against him— he was in a situation that didn't honor him but presented him as cheap, worthless—something not to be respected. So, the big man in Egypt said, "Make his stay honorable among us. Maybe, he will bring us much good, or we shall adopt him as our son." Now look what G-d says, "Thus did we establish Joseph in the land." Now this was the reasoning of the big man in Egypt—in the strange land where Joseph has fallen. Joseph has finally fallen into the strange land in Egypt.

A powerful land—the most powerful land of that time. There was no other land more powerful than Egypt at that time. Now Joseph had fallen into the hands of the Egyptians after being put into the dark hole and sold into slavery. The big chief in Egypt, he saw value in Joseph. He said to his wife (his wife is like the Queen; she is a big woman - the big man had a big wife) "Make his stay honorable. Maybe he will bring much good or we shall adopt him as a son." And G-d said "Thus"—meaning on that fashion—"Did we establish Joseph in the land, that we might teach him."

G-d put him into a situation where G-d can teach him. "That we might teach him the interpretation of stories or events." Now why was Egypt a good situation for Joseph to learn the interpretation of stories and events? It is because Egypt was a land that was heavily in its culture— heavily symbolic—great symbolism.

Reading on the symbolic, mystical language of Egyptian culture, I read where in their myth, in their mythology there was an oracle. An oracle is a mysterious thing that holds prophecy. There was an oracle that would speak to anyone that was trying to enter Egypt. If you tried to enter Egypt, you had to first be addressed by this oracle. The oracle would ask you a riddle or give a riddle, and you had to interpret that riddle correctly. If you didn't interpret that riddle correctly, you couldn't get into Egypt.

Now mind you, Egypt was the baddest and the biggest, and the most important land or nation in existence at that time. It had great science, great army, great power, great ruling order-- and respect in the known world then as being the superpower, Egypt at that time. The name Cairo, qahira is the capitol of Egypt—the main city in Egypt. Its name means subduing—just overcoming, just overwhelming. Something that puts you in awe—holds you spellbound. That is what the name means. If you ever visited Egypt like some of us did—some of our pioneers, Sheikh Shabazz and I, many of us, several of us, a group of us, we made a trip to Egypt upon invitation. The Egyptian government invited us to come.

So, we made a trip to Egypt there. We saw huge statues of their ancient rulers, and the buildings, the kind of structures that they lived in. They are still there preserved. The doorway is so huge that if you came from another land on their land and were suddenly brought in the doorway of their people, you would be frightened to death, because you would be expecting a man to walk through there about maybe twenty feet tall—huge doors, huge doorways. The statues of them are very huge, standing as high as this building here, as high as this auditorium—the statues of their great ones.

Their language was the language of symbols. The ancient Egyptians called it hieroglyphics. It is the language of symbols. Where we speak now with words, they spoke with symbols. We read now words in print. They read symbols. Whatever they wanted to say they had symbol for it. Whether it was a sunrise, or a bird, or a broken stick, or a fast running animal, they had some symbol to say what they wanted to say. They were not backwards. They were not primitive. They were most advanced. So advanced that the best of our scientists from the West are still trying hard to decipher their wisdom. They have been doing it now for many, many decades. In fact if you go over there you will see curious students—men of learning over there right now at the Cairo museum trying to break codes, decipher the wisdom of those ancient people. They are still doing it.

They were doing it when I was over there and I am sure they are still doing it now. They haven't stopped. Egypt, unlike most ancient nations, has a whole science called Egyptology. There are books and books, volumes called Egyptology. Now here is a nation that was so great that they had to make a whole course, a study just for that nation—Egyptology. Yes, it was great in its science and great in its mysteries.

Another note we should make right now is that of the scripture of the people of this particular part of the world, Bible. It warns them, of a time coming when there would be an appearance of a nation and a people, just like that called modern Egypt. You have ancient Babylon, modern Babylon; ancient Egypt, modern Egypt. "So we might teach him the interpretations of stories or events." G-d would teach him the tahweel.

G-d would teach him the interpretation of some of the stories and events. "And G-d has full power and control over his affairs, but most among mankind know it not." The situation for a people can never become so bad, so hopeless that they can't be saved by G-d. "When Joseph attained his full manhood, we gave him power and knowledge. Thus do we reward those who do right. The word for those who do right is the plural "muhsineen"— the doers of good. Joseph was one who practiced goodness.

Now, the big lady, she was fascinated by Joseph. And this verse says, "But she, in whose house he was, sought to seduce him from his true self". And the expression in Qur'anic language is "an-nafsi" which means from his true nature, his true self just as it is given here. Now here you have a picture of an innocent victim, young when he was taken—right? He was a "ghulam" very young, young lad. He was young when he was taken. He was taken and put in bad circumstances by his own brethren who plotted against him. G-d says that there was something of great value in Joseph, but they didn't respect that value in him.

The treated him as though he was something mean and cheap. Here now we have favorable circumstances coming about wherein the big man in Egypt takes him into his own care and puts him in the house where the big lady was. Now, here the big lady of the house, she is enamored by him. She now wants to seduce him, take him out of his true nature. So, obviously his true nature was that of a righteous person. He was a virtuous person. I am sure it wouldn't take a lot of you out of your true nature if a beautiful big lady wanted to go to sleep with you tonight, but for Joseph this was a threat to his very good nature, to his true self. That was not his self, to allow the woman to seduce him. She fastened the doors and said, "Now come thou dear one!" He said, "G-d forbid, truly thy husband is my lord. He made my sojourn agreeable. Truly no good comes to those who do wrong."

So he was aware of the consequences. He was aware of
his obligation. He was aware that he was indebted to a
man who favored him and trusted him, and he was aware
that wrong begets wrong and bad consequences. It is not
only that I owe this to him—not to betray him behind his
back, but I owe it to myself to keep my own good nature.
If I lose it, I will fall into worse circumstances. This is a
beautiful story! And to read it in Arabic is even more
beautiful. More of us insha-Allah will learn Arabic.

"And with passion did she desire him. And he would have
desired her except that he saw the evidence of his Lord."
He was conscious of G-d—that is what saved him. So
what are we being told here? That he was human like she
was. If it wasn't for divine protection, he would have been
right into the same thing that she was weak for. So for a
people who are put in circumstances like that, their only
protection is the fear of G-d. Once they lose the fear of G-
d, they are finished. "Thus did we order that we might
turn away from him all evil and shameful deeds." So here
G-d orders this test for him. G-d ordered a test for him, to

try him, to put him a situation to make his muscles of resistance and devotion to G-d stronger.

See if you are good, your intentions are good, your commitment is righteous and honorable, then the more temptation you are put into, the stronger you become. Sometimes the young person in his virtuous life, he needs to be put into situations that will bring out that strength that is in him, because once he says no to the big lady, he won't have much trouble saying no to the little ladies. So G-d wanted to hurry and prepare Joseph to survive. So he didn't give him the little ladies first. He gave him the big lady first. So to get it over quick, if you can stand the big lady, you will make it among the little ladies.

Now this story of Joseph is very mystical itself. It is a mystical story, a very mythical story. So we are to receive understanding on levels—understanding on one level may not be the same understanding for a higher level. So now we are thinking about the carnal weakness—the weaknesses of the flesh. The flesh is being put to the test; but there are higher levels upon which we are tested too—

right? He said, "It was she who sought to seduce me from my true self." One of her household witnessed this and said if it be that his shirt is torn from the front then he is the liar but if it be that his shirt is torn from the back then she is the liar and he is telling the truth. So when he saw that his shirt was torn from the back her husband said "behold it is a snare of your women; truly mighty is your snare. The big chief had a lady who would set traps. He didn't like that in her but obviously accepted that in her. He was tolerating her with that in her. "Oh Joseph pass this over" he said "oh wife, ask forgiveness for your sin for truly thou has been at fault." So this kind of snare or trap setting of hers is not accepted being right

Do you know that you are constantly being seduced by the powers of the land? They are constantly trying to seduce you out of your true self. Now they may think that G-d allows that they work these schemes, plots against the good nature that G-d created, but G-d says here it is a sin, and one who is guilty of it should pray for forgiveness. That didn't get Joseph out of the situation. He was still in that situation. She said to the ladies that also desired him very passionately that there before you is the man about whom you did blame me. When they saw him, they got into the same fix, but they had blamed the big lady for being weak. She said, "I did seek to seduce him from his true self. But, he did firmly save himself guiltless, and now if he does not do my bidding, he shall certainly be cast into prison; and what is more, he will be in the company of the vilest (meaning those who are low and debased)."

Here is a situation used to throw us among people who are among the lowest. So, obviously Joseph in his excellence as a person, as a human being—he was very, very, very great in his virtuous life. He was very great. He was on a high standard. His value was his obedience to what is right. His value was moral value. His value was the virtuous life. That was his value. Now if a people are thrown into such circumstances, if they lose their moral excellence, their moral tenacity, their moral endurance, the moral consistency in their life—wherein they hold to what is right—if they lose that, they lose their value. They don't have any other value. What value has the African-American in his situation? He cannot compete politically. He can not compete economically. He has no established

ethnicity. So where is our value if it is not in moral
consistency? Once we lose moral consistency, we have no
worth as a people. We don't measure up anywhere. But
for a long time that moral consistency in our life made us
the envy of white people that stood above us in every other
way. But, in the last fifteen or twenty years, we have lost
our precious value. That value gave us a sense of worth
and made us the envy of many people who had the things
of this world. G-d was with us.

Yes, G-d was with us, but not anymore. No, not any more.
Don't think G-d is with the Black man—not anymore.
The Black man has lost the favor of G-d by turning around
right at the crucial moment when he could have saved
himself totally. He turned around and picked up the ways
of the wicked and let his whole race fall under the
influence of the wicked. Yes, it is a shame. So no more.
It is going to take a very small number from among us to
complete the work, because the majority is finished. They
are out of it.

Now, in the prison situation—he was put in a favorable situation by the big man in Egypt. Now, because he wouldn't go along with the deceit of the big lady, he is cast out of that good situation; now back into a bad situation. Now he is among those who are imprisoned. Isn't that the ways of the great powers? Yes, it is the ways of the great powers. They will give you freedom for an advantage for them, and as soon as you begin to show an independent mind, they want to lock you up. You know, you don't have to be in the physical boundaries of physical measurements... walls, prison walls, to be in prison. The people who have an independent moral mind in Chicago today are imprisoned.

They will not allow you to be free. I know because I am one of you. They deny us freedom. You might say well Imam how can you say that, you are free. You are down here in the mosque saying all of this. But they spend hundreds of thousands of dollars to make sure that I have this audience, and that it doesn't get any bigger. Yes, so now he is cast into a bad situation again, but the good is like a mighty seed. If there is a situation for it to burst into life, it will. So, even in the prison situation, the mighty attributes of Joseph are manifested. There were those who needed his help and he became a helper to them. The big people outside in the free world Egypt, they learned of his help that he was giving inmates and they desired that help for the free. They said bring him up out of prison. We need him. We are in trouble too.

Now don't forget what G-d said when He allowed Joseph to fall into those circumstances and be taken up by the powerful people. He said, "Thus did We establish Joseph in the land." Now in the prison there came to him two young men. Said one of them, "I see myself in a dream pressing wine." Said the other, "I see myself in a dream carrying bread on my head and birds are eating thereof." "Tell us," they said, "the truth and meaning thereof for we see thou art one that is good to all (that's Joseph)." They said, "we are imprisoned here, we don't know you Joseph. We are strangers and convicts. But we know that you are a person that does good by all. So help us with our situation."

He said, "Before any food come in the due course to feed either of you, I will surely reveal to you the truth and meaning of this that will befall you. That is part of the duty which my Lord has taught me, I assure you. Abandon the ways of a people that believe not in G-d and even deny the hereafter."

Now, listen, he was a small lad when he came into the bad circumstances, right? His own brethren put him into the bad circumstances. Then in the bad circumstances, the big man of the land saw good in him. So much that he said, "Let's take him because there may be some great good in him for us. Or maybe we will adopt him as our own son." Obviously, they did adopt him as their own son. Why? Because he says, "Now, I have turned from the ways of a people that believe not in G-d and deny the hereafter." He was a young lad. He was not experienced in the world to know what was happening. But because of his moral tenacity, moral strength and endurance, he held his moral life together. He wouldn't let anything take it apart. Because of that being in him, G-d was with him all of the time. Isn't that wonderful? G-d aided him at every turn of the events. No matter how bad the circumstances,

G-d was with him. Now he is talking to inmates in prison with him, in another bad situation and he tells them that "I have abandoned the ways of a people who believe not."

When did he take on wrong beliefs? He didn't have wrong beliefs when his brothers took him. He was with his father. He was just young. He didn't have knowledge and insight. He was just young. But he didn't have any false beliefs. The sign that he didn't have any false beliefs was the charge of animal blood being on his shirt. The old man said, "I don't believe that. That boy wouldn't do anything like that. That boy doesn't mess around with any animals." So where did he get that wrong belief? He got the wrong belief in that good situation with the powerful people of the land.

Where did we get our wrong beliefs? Where did we get our shirk? Where did we get our idolatry? Didn't we get it when they said you are free now to have your Christianity just like we have our Christianity? Then we became guilty of believing in more then one G-d, of saying G-d has a son who is G-d and there are three G-ds. That is when we came into that. Like Joseph, when we stood up and declared the true belief in G-d, they put us in prison. When we were guilty of shirk, they put us on Sixty minutes; they put us on prime time television. They told the whole world our message and showed us respect. They even tried to justify our hate by saying, "The hate that hate produced." In other words, They are not guilty of that hate. Hate has produced their hate. We admire their militancy. We admire their discipline. We admire them for their cleanliness. Oh they are like us.

They say that man is G-d and they don't believe in a hereafter. These are truly our boys. They don't want our women. Take note, we favor these negros over those integrationists. But as soon as we stood up under the influence of our moral nature and said, "Hey, this is the true Islam. That was false Islam" then they said, "Hey lock him up in prison. Cast him with the vilest - Jim Jones and others."

He called them his companions. Isn't that a wonderful man? He knew of his excellence, but in the prison, he

looked at the circumstances of those in prison with him.
He wanted to help them. He helped them and called them
his companions; his companions in that situation. He said,
"I follow the ways of my fathers, Abraham, Isaac, and
Jacob and never could we attribute any partners
whatsoever to G-d. That comes of the grace of G-d to us
and to mankind. Yet most men are not grateful."

Now look! These twelve, Israel were supposed to be the
favorites, right? Israel, because after all according to the
western people in the religion, they say that Jacob became
Israel—and Israel is the favorite—the favored and that no
one can get the special blessings that G-d has for Israel
except through Israel. You have to get it from Israel. You
can't get it from G-d. You have to get it by coming
through Israel, and you cannot be called one by
inheritance. You will be one by adoption. Don't forget
that!

Now, what does our book say of this special group? It
says, "That comes of the grace of G-d to us and to
mankind." It is not just to us, but G-d favors all men as he

favors us. Do you see that? Most of us would miss that. "On us and on all people." So, here is Joseph—he is the true one. Joseph, he can't lie. Joseph says, "Yes, this special gift that you see now in me—it has come through our ancestors down to me. But it is not just for us. It is for all people." He said, "O my two companions of the prison, I ask you, are many lords differing among themselves better; or is the one Lord, Supreme and Irresistible?"

So, here the attributes that they put on Egypt—the Subduer—are changed a bit to make it a more powerful subduer, and it is given as the name of our G-d, Al Qahhar. Qahhirah is Egypt—meaning it is something that makes it seem that you are under a spell. It captivates you and subdues you, and here is the name of our G-d given now—more powerful than that—Al Qahhar. He is the Subduer. That is to tell Egypt—you can't subdue. G-d is the Subduer. Yea, you try to subdue them. You are going to wash out their conscience. You are going to drown their conscience. You are going to drown their senses.

Well, there is One that is powerful enough to drown you out. Wasn't that the fate of Pharaoh and his hosts? They got drowned in the sea—though he called himself the lord. He said, "I recognize no god but me." That is what Pharaoh said. I wonder how he sounded when that water was going down his throat. Joseph continues now, "O my two companions of the prison, I ask you, "are many lords differing among themselves better than the one G-d, Supreme and Irresistible?'

Now we are told in Christianity or by the Christians that actually the three are three in one. But, we are told also that they differ. They are three in one, and yet they differ. How do they differ? The father is the G-d as conceived or presented in the Old Testament. The son is the god as conceived or presented in the New Testament. If they were the same, they wouldn't have asked for a new god? They are different. The G-d of the Old Testament is not like the god of the New Testament, they are different.

Now here are gods differing with one another. Now that is like one coming from fascist rule. One man who used to rule the land, or a particular people, or a world was a fascist. He was a cruel man. He used power in a brutal way. Then they change now and send another—and he says, "My image is spoiled in the world. Now I am going to have a son that is not like me. He is going to be just the other extreme. Now I am firm. Now he is going to be forgiving. As I have been firm to the extreme, he is going to be forgiving to the extreme. As I have been so firm to the extreme that I have castrated men because they messed over my faithful ones; just as I have gone to the extreme—I have burned up nations.

I have set fire over them. I have just licked up worlds with fire. I am going to present one now that is going to be the other extreme. As I have been firm and strict to the extreme, this one is going to be mild and forgiving to the extreme. So forgiving, the he is going to accept them to crucify him, kill him, and he is going to say, "I forgive you."

Now, you are going to tell me they are not different. They are different. Those two purported gods are not the same.

They are different; and the choice of the child over the father is because the old image was rejected. They rejected the old image of god. So if god the father is not in the bad image, he is good—how did he become good? He became good by repenting, when he decided to introduce himself through his son. That would be the other extreme—the mild lord. When he decided that, he repented from his old ways and became the new man. So these are still different gods. So you say, "Well the father he is good just like the son. He is the son". Well, if he is the son, what was he before? So through his son, he has repented. The son not only has become the savior of the world, the son has become the savior of the image of his father. There is no way to get around that. So, they are different.

Now, here comes the Holy Ghost in Christianity—still different. Jesus, he accepted all kinds of abuses. "But the Gospel says "You bring this attitude to the Holy Ghost, it won't be forgiven." That is what it says. You can do these things to the son, but to the Holy Ghost, if you do it, it will not be forgiven. So, there is still another one that is different. The first one is adamant, is not accepting to bow or bend to anything. Then the son is coming—so sweet. Now here comes the Holy Ghost—"I don't take any stuff either. I am a mystery, but I don't take any stuff. Now don't play with me like you played with the son." So these are different. I am not making a joke. Believe me; I don't have any spirit to joke with this. They are different! And that is what Allah is telling us in the revelation to Muhammad (pbuh). He is telling us by way of hints and allusions, that these Christian Trinitarian ideas–they claim as one--and god is three in one—but they have differing gods. They are not three in one. They are not all the same. They are differing with each other.

Muslims, you must understand! Many of us are so recent—right from the Holy Ghost session. We come in and say, "I am a Muslim. My name is Rasheed Hameed. And I am a Muslim now." But we still have the conditioning from the church life. We get over here and we think, "They believe basically the same as we do." You are wrong. "And we are to respect their beliefs." You are wrong.

We are to respect their goodness. We are to respect their innocence. We are not to respect their falsehoods. By that I mean we are not to go to a church and make them feel uncomfortable, attacking what they believe in. But if we think they are sensible enough, sober enough in their minds and hearts to stand for us to read Qur'an concerning their troubles–their trouble spots in their beliefs—we should have the courage to go to the church and read Qur'an to them.

Allah says in this Qur'an, highly glorified is He—He says to the people of the book, "Cease, stop saying three. It will be better for you if you only understood." So, Allah is not tolerating their belief in three in one. It is plainly said. "Stop that!" Now you are Muslims. Some of you say you are responsible for the Dawah, for inviting the people to this religion. So what are you going to do? Are you going to go out there and tell them it is OK to believe in that; god is three in one? Or will you tell them what Allah says in the Qur'an? "Cease, stop doing that. It is best if you only understood." That should be your message to the church. To go to them and tell them, "Look! You have a confusion here. Stop this. It is best for you if you only understood."

Tell them what G-d says in your book! And maybe you will earn the favor G-d back on your people.

Joseph continues now, he says, "O my two companions of the prison as to one of you—he will pour out the wine for his lord to drink." Now haven't we been as a religious people pouring out the wine for our lord to drink? Think about it! Just until recently—and many of us are still doing it. It is not as strong as it used to be. But the church leadership is trying to recuperate. They are reviving, and they pour out wine for their lord to drink—don't they?

Their congregation gets drunk but their lord drinks. Their lord is down at city hall, in Springfield, and the big industrialists. Those are the lords that enjoy the drink of wine that they pour out. That is all the Christianity message that they give to the poor blacks. That is all that they give to the poor Hispanics. The Christianity that they give to the poor and ignorant people—is nothing but alcoholism. They get you all drunk in the head, drunk in the mind, where you don't care about anything other than death. Just like a dope addict gets hooked on dope and he doesn't care about anything but the dope. An alcoholic gets hooked on alcohol; he cares about nothing but the alcohol. Some of our people are drinking the alcoholism of Christianity; get hooked on it and care about nothing but the alcohol. It is the same thing. The neighborhood is going to waste. Life is going to waste. The community is not going anywhere. It is being taken advantage of and exploited.

They don't worry about those things. Just give me another drink. "You will pour out the wine for his lord to drink. As for the other he will hang from the cross." So either you are going to pour out the wine or you are going to be hanging on the cross. If you don't pour out the wine, you've got to hang from the cross. And I guarantee you that is the situation for the people of conscience; the poor struggling people of conscience... If they don't join the deceitful order of these fraternities, these secret fraternities and hypocrites in religion; if they don't join them and pour the wine, fill the cup with the wine—they are going to be crucified.

Crucified means deprived of your freedom to the extent
that you can't move anything. The limbs that you depend
upon to support you and to carry you and to work for you
are crucified. It's like rigor mortis has set in. "And the
birds will eat from his head. So has been decreed that
matter whereof you twain do inquire." So Joseph became
one that was sought as a way out of trouble and as a person
that could bring understanding and relief.

Do you remember how white people used to write about
how our parents–mothers and fathers—helped them solve
great problems, brought great relief to them? Rulers in
this part of the world, rich people in this part of the
world—have written in their memoirs how our poor
ignorant folks brought them understanding and great relief
and helped them out of bad situations—gave them light to
go by. We were good at heart, we were innocent, we were
morally upright. Though we were in the bottom of the pit,
the dark hole, or cast into prison, G-d was with us. Our
value was there and it was recognized by great people at
many turns of events.

You should think about these things, and get your life again or make it stronger. Make your commitment stronger. If you still have it, make it stronger. "And of the two, to that one whom he considered about to be saved, he said, 'mention me to thy lord'; but Satan made him forget to mention him to his lord and Joseph lingered in prison for a few more years." Now, here Joseph has helped one of the inmates. He told one of the inmates after he had helped him, "When you get to your lord, mention me. Let your lord know the situation that I am in." Showing how cold the world can become, even the best people fail you. These people recognized the goodness in Joseph and they were trying to find a way out of the bad life. Joseph helped them and when he told him, "now when you get in a good situation, mention me to your lord." He got in a good situation and forgot to mention to his chief, the boss—that there is a good man down there in prison. Your ladies have put him away for good. He was a good man.

Why didn't he put in a word for Joseph? He was so much occupied by his own interest that he couldn't remember the man that helped him, relieved him when he was in this bad situation too. Now, think of ourselves as a people.

Don't you know many of your grandparents, your grandmothers and fathers and relatives-many of them told us to remember them. Saying, "Now look! Freedom is going to come one day. Now when you are freed, remember us." But freedom came and we became so much overcome by our own desires to please our own selves right now, immediately, right here—that we forgot them.

We should be remembering them to our Lord, to G-d "O G-d, have mercy on the souls of our ancestors. They were in the dark, they were oppressed and they wanted to see the daylight. O, G-d, forgive them for whatever sins they did and admit them into Your paradise." But instead of remembering them to our Lord, we indulged into foolishness and self destruction—just for a quick thrill. So, that is what we are doing, aren't we? Pouring wine or crucifying.

Now we will begin with the same section here, section six of this chapter on Joseph and continue the talk and pray G-d it strengthens us, shine some light on our situation. But remember this! G-d says that, "That is how he established Joseph in the land". Now if we find in our circumstances as an enslaved people, kept subdued people in this part of the world; if we find in our circumstances events similar to those that were in the life of Joseph and if we believe in the word of G-d, the Qur'an—then we should take hints from that story and strengthen our life. Look! We do not have economic power. We don't have political power. We are not favored in this country. Now, you can make yourself believe whatever you want to believe. You can just drift out there in the world of make believe. That is up to you. But, I am talking reality. We are not favored in this country. We are the disfavored in this country.

Our circumstances are still bad. Then take the hints from that story. Say now G-d will establish us if we keep our moral tenacity. G-d will establish us if we are morally consistent. If we would want right by everybody, if we would want good for everybody, not just for Blacks, but for everybody. Here a people in slavery and a people freed, so called liberated. And for all the time they were trying to get equal opportunity or get into the mainstream of these United States or the life of America—they were claiming that they had a belief in a G-d, and that they had a belief in moral justice, Divine justice. They were claiming to be good people. Wasn't that our claim? As a race, our politicians and our religious people, our church people were speaking in the name of all of us—and they were claiming before the world that we are a G-d fearing people that believe in the moral justice of G-d. Then as soon as we got the freedom that we wanted to play and have some ice cream cones, and some hot dogs, and chili. As soon as we got that freedom to play and have some common food, we forgot what it was all about. We forgot the moral message that we sent out. We betrayed it right in our own life so soon. You see why we aren't getting anywhere now?

So, let's pray for forgiveness; and take hints from that great, mystical, beautiful passage, story in the Qur'an of Joseph. Take hints from it to strengthen and tighten up your own life and your own situation. So we pray G-d forgive us our sins, strengthen our faith, make pure our intentions, and establish us among the good and excellent followers of Muhammad, the Prophet—peace and the blessings be upon him. AMEEN.

It is in English as given by the international scholar
Abdullah Yusuf. He gives Al-fatihah, it means the
opening, the opening chapter. And it reads, "With G-d's
name, Most Gracious, Most Merciful. Praise be to G-d,
the Cherisher and Sustainer of the worlds. Most Gracious,
Most Merciful. Master of the day of judgment. Thee do
we worship and thine aid we seek. Show us the straight
way. The way of those on whom, you bestow grace.
Those whose portion is not wrath and who go not astray.
Ameen".

We will read now from the seventh chapter of Qur'an,
Chapter the heights, Al-araf in Arabic. The word Al-araf
translated means, "the Heights". It literally means in its
root meaning, heights, knowledge wise. It comes from the
root word "arafa" which means 'to know". Al-araf means
the greatest extensions or elevation of knowledge and it is
called the heights by the translator. However, the verse
that we are going to read gives us the full range of the
message of Muhammad, the Prophet, the peace and the
blessings be on him, as to what people or what race or

what nation, he came to guide or came to give G-d's revelation to. Verse 158 of this chapter reads, "Say O men,"

And in the language of Qur'an, the Arabic language of Qur'an, this language in Arabic is call Fusha, Arabiya Fusha. It is the standard of the language for all colleges, universities, etc. It set the standard for the highest institutions in the Islamic world. It is the highest standard of the Arabic Language. In fact, the fusha is formed because of the Qur'an. It is formed by the guidelines of the Qur'an, the fusha, means the highest standard of Arabic. And many of you who are learning Arabic to read Qur'an, you are learning fusha. And if you speak that, many of us say "I have learned some words. I am going to show some people that I speak Arabic". It is only natural. You go and speak to an Arab in the language fusha and he will have difficulties understanding you. Most of them would be happy to know that you are learning Qur'an in Arabic, fusha. Only the sinners among the Arabs will not be happy. But all of the Arabs, almost would be happy to know that you are learning Arabic, the Qur'anic Arabic, the Arabic of our holy book. But, most of them would not be able to understand fusha when it is spoken as a language. The common language of the people has not been fusha for many, many, many hundreds of years now. They have left that. And they have dialects of Arabic, colloquial language, the common language, colloquial, it means the language that is spoken in a particular area. So, we have that over there, like in Egypt, they will speak different from the people in Iraq and they will speak different then the people in Saudi Arabia, and so it will go you see.

And when you go to a market and you speak fusha, the very best Arabic which is the Qur'an. In fact the Qur'an sets the standard for fusha. Many stupid people over there will snicker. They will even laugh. And they won't be making mockery of you, but it will be funny to them that you are speaking so proper and many times they can't even understand it. Like here in the United States, we say we speak English, right? But, if we speak pure English, people will laugh at us. They will say, "hey, where did he come from?" We speak American English. It is not pure English. And even if we speak proper American English, some people will laugh at us. You have to speak the common language of the people. So, it is with Arabic, only with Arabic it is more like the situation for the Italian people. Italian people, they speak Italian. But, Latin is the old language. And Latin now still set the stage for the other Latin languages. Like Italian and the others. But, it is called a dead language. Some of you should make note right there. It is called a dead language. But, yet, though it is dead, it is still holding the other Latin languages to the line. So, a similar kind of thing has happened in the Muslim Land. The Qur'an was revealed in pure Arabic, the best Arabic.

But as time passed, the Muslims have drifted away from the purity of their language and there are now many local languages that are Arabic but not pure Arabic. And I believe this is the instigation of the Satan, the devil to take the people away from the language of their knowledge source. The Qur'an is the knowledge source. He encouraged them to get away from the language, their knowledge source, so it will be hard for them to understand their knowledge source. So, many Arabs, they can't understand the Qur'an as well as you can. And, it is because they don't know the fusha either.

A few of them will know the fusha, only those who come up in the Islamic schools or come up under Islamic tutoring and receive instructions in Qur'an or Islamic Studies, only they will understand the Qur'anic language. But, you will read it to them and they will hear it and you will be thinking that they know it. No! They can understand a little because they are Arabs, so they understand a little, it touches their hearts, they understand a little. But there is much that they will be missing because they don't know themselves the Qur'anic high standard language of the Qur'an. And I guess that account for much of the weak faith in the Islamic world. Because if they don't know, how can they have strong faith. That is not the way of Al-Islam.

What I mean by that, Prophet Muhammad (pbuh) did not set that example, he did not teach them anything that would give them a reason to fall into patterns like that. In the days of the Prophet, the teaching of this Qur'an was for everybody. It was for everybody. In fact, it was the source of knowledge for what we may call the religious and secular world. There was no such thing as religious and secular world in the time of Muhammad, the Prophet, peace and blessings be on him. There was only one united world. And the full light for the whole society, religion, science, education, government, politics, whatever, all was derived from careful study of Qur'an and the teachings of Muhammad, the Prophet, the peace be upon him. The school of sciences that came immediately after the preaching of this Qur'an by Muhammad (pbuh), they were first students of Qur'an and they based all of their great findings on the revealing light of the Qur'an. We are told that they rediscovered the sciences, the great sciences of the ancient Greeks, Aristotle and others.

That is true. But, it was not only the ancient Greeks, there were others too. It just so happen that the west is more interested in the sciences of the ancient Greeks. But what Persia had in its great history before and other great empires and nations, Muslims were also interested in that. And they brought all of that science to be respected again. Prophet Muhammad (pbuh) said to go even to the far country of China in search of knowledge So, he didn't limit their intellect. He didn't limit their intellectual curiosity. But, he taught them that their intellectual curiosity should be free and that they should go wherever knowledge is. Seek it! Seek it to verify your position, not to just follow it blindly, but seek it to verify your position. So, if we understand this religion and understand Muhammad, the Prophet, peace be upon him, the Muslim is the free-est and the most consistent man on this earth. If he would just be what he is supposed to be, the free-est and the most consistent.

So, here G-d says in this verse. "Say, O men, I am sent unto you all as the apostle of G-d. to Whom belong the dominion of the heavens and the earth. There is no G-d but he. It is he who giveth both life and death. So, believe in G-d and in his Apostle, the unlettered Prophet (pbuh)." Unlettered means uneducated. It also means for Muslims that he could not read. But to say that a man is a lettered man in English means he is an educated man. To say he is unlettered in English means he is not educated. I will continue to read this verse now until its conclusion.

It continues, "Who believes in G-d and His words", then the command comes, that is my expression now and I continue now, "follow him that you may be guided." The focus here is on Muhammad (pbuh) as a messenger of G-d to all people. "Say, O men I am sent unto you all as the Apostle of G-d. Apostle is another term for messenger of G-d. And in Arabic, Qul ya-ayuhan-nas is translated as "O men" because English also uses men to mean all men. Man means all men also. So, in religious language, even in English, terms like man and men can mean all people. If you look in the dictionary, you will find that meaning under one of the entries for the definition, for the definition, you will find that meaning in the dictionary, for man and men. It can refer to all men or man by itself, singular. It refers to all men like the expression mankind.

The word in Arabic is An-nas. An-nas means the people. An-nas means all the people. There is no such word as An-nas for Blacks, or An-nas for Chinese. An-nas is for all people. That term is for all people. So, An-nas means all the people. "Say O people", speaking to all the people, "surely I am." G-d is telling Muhammad (pbuh) to say

this. "surely I am a messenger of G-d to you" (plural).
Kum means you plural, "to all of you."

So, there is no question as to the people that G'd sent
Muhammad (pbuh) to, who they are, whether they are
Arabs, Blacks, Whites, Mongolian, or African. No! All
people, it is very clearly stated, "Say to the people, Surely,
I am the Messenger of G-d to you, all of you," not
excluding anybody.

Say, "What G-d is this?" "I won't follow the Arab god. I
am not going to follow no Arab idol god!" So, what god is
it? It is not the Arab god. It is not the god of Israel. It is
not Israeli god. It is not Arab god. It is not black god.
Says al-lathe, "to whom", al-lathe lahu, "to whom belongs"
mulkus-samawatee, "the dominion of the skies" which is
translated heavens.

Now if you tell anybody that the G-d, the power,
Muhammad (pbuh) represented is the One that is
responsible for the order and rule of all that you see up in

the sky, and on earth. La ilaha illa huwa, "there is no other G-d except Him" yuhyee wa yumeet, "he gives life and gives death" fa aminu bil-lahi wa rasulihin-nabiyil umiy-yil-lathe yu'minu bil-lahi wa kalimatihi, "therefore believe in G-d and in his messenger, the unlettered prophet, who himself believes in G-d". He is no hypocrite.

He is nobody who trying to dupe the spiritual world into coming into a spiritual bag and he is going to work his thing over their heads, like many have done to the masses of the world. It is very clear that this man is not one who has a game for the fools and he himself is not believing or taking the same medicine or following the same prescription that he is giving the masses. No! He believes in G-d. He is a man of faith. And in another place in the Qur'an, it says, "we have hear a caller, calling to faith", that was the way Prophet Muhammad (pbuh) was first seen as a man calling people to faith.

To believe in G-d first of all, to believe in His messenger, to believe in the last of the messengers, Muhammad (pbuh) himself. "Who believes in G-d and in His word, he

believes in G-d and he believes in the revelation, the
scripture. Wat-tabi-oo-hu. "and follow him" meaning "and
follow Muhammad (pbuh)." La-ala-kum tah-ta-dun, "in
order for you to be guided right," this is clear enough for
Muslims. Is this clear enough? It should be. It should be
clear enough that our Prophet, Muhammad, the peace be
upon him, he is the messenger who was sent from Allah,
the last messenger, not to one people, but to all people on
earth, for all times, not just for then, but for all times, for
all times in the future to come.

He is the completion of prophethood, he is the last of the
messengers. This not in any general kind of vision, or in a
general kind of sense. This is in a specific sense. So, G-d
had a plan in the very beginning to give the people that he
created what they need for their health and their guidance
in their whole life. And he gave it out in degrees or in
portions according to the situation, the circumstances, he
gave it out. And he had in his great plan to advance the
people on this earth by step by step gradual assistance until
he bring them into the full life of what life they should
have on this planet as one people, not as different people;
as one people. And when that comes, there is no giving in

to any pressure to put that behind something else. That can't take a subordinate role in the world behind something else.

That kind of universal message intended by G-d cannot be second to anything. It cannot be second to any ideology. It cannot sit back and let secularism take over the life of man. No! Those who truly receive and understand the clear guidance of this Holy Book, they know that this vision is the leading vision for man on this earth. And this religion, is the highest idea and the highest concept for the life of man on this earth. And this religion is intended by G-d, Himself, to prevail over other ideologies and religions though the enemies of it hate it or detest it according to the word of G-d in this Holy Book. So, let us clearly see the light and let us be ourselves in the light.

Some of us will not be able to respect the obligation established in the light. Some of us will be too weak. We will carry seventy percent of the load, another will carry eighty percent, another will carry ninety, another will carry maybe all of the load that he possibly can, and some will only carry thirty percent of the load. Some will carry nothing. But, let us at least do justice to our own good senses. Let us not close our eyes foolishly to what G-d is saying to Muslims and to the world in this Holy Book, the last revelation.

He is saying to us that this is His plan for human beings on this earth. It was sent expressly to be plain and clear according to the words in the Qur'an. It was not sent to be put into esoterics, to be put into symbolism, to be put into cryptology, or any other hard language to decipher or decode. It was sent to be taught plainly, openly, and clearly, according to the words of G-d in this book. And it is wonderful to see... and you won't see unless G-d blesses you with it. It is wonderful to see as a student of the Qur'an that the Qur'an gives us the symbols, it gives us the esoterics, it gives us language in allegory, in picture form.

The same book also gives us that in clear, plain, simple language. Yes! This is a marvelous book. And, I use that expression because I don't have a better one right now, a divine book, a wonderful book. That, that is hidden is given, but whatever is hidden is also revealed for the plain common man, by this book. So, when you read the whole Qur'an don't think that you are missing anything. If you read the whole Qur'an and you just have common man sense, you don't have the tools of interpretation, you only have common man sense.

You don't have the fraternal keys. You just have the common man sense. Be assured that when you read this whole Qur'an, you haven't missed anything. Because, whatever they hid, G-d gave it again in another language so you can get it. The only thing that you missed is how they get it. You get it. But, they only thing you miss is how the secret people get it, their language, their tricks, their double talk, their play on concepts. You miss their game thing, but you don't miss what G-d intended for the people, because G-d has given it in plain language. That is why they are not happy to see this book in the hands of the ordinary people.

There use to be a time that if they see any of us, African Americans, I have to say indigenous African Americans, because I said this overseas, and they said "African American?", they thought we meant the people from Africa living in America. So, I guess that is why it never caught on. African-American, I guess it never caught on because nothing can really be fully established in a nation without being accepted at least pretty well in the international world. So, we can call ourselves African-Americans and all that forever, but unless that is understood in the international world, it is going to be a problem for us establishing it here as a way of addressing ourselves as our race.

So, I see the problem now; so I said at least when I write books, I am going to have to not say African-American or Afro-American, I am going to have to say indigenous. They understand that indigenous to mean us. That word has caught on overseas. When we say indigenous Blacks, they understand that to mean us. So, indigenous has caught on. And you will be happy to know that indigenous has caught on also in the international Muslim circles for our efforts here to come into the right religion or the right light of Al-Islam.

They refer to us who came from the Honorable Elijah Muhammad's leadership, into the sunnah, into the standard religion now; they refer to us as the Indigenous American Muslims. And they are watching us with great hope and great anticipation. They are not so excited about the immigrant Muslims as they are excited about what they call The Indigenous American Muslims. And indigenous means forming with the land. You formed with the land. And I was talking to a young girl, Muslim girl of our community about this. In fact, it was about five days ago. And, she said, "You know I have always felt that I was just an American. Now, isn't that something? She said, "I always felt that I was just an American." Now, I wasn't agreeing with her altogether, but I was happy to hear her say that, because I think of myself as a Muslim American. And I think of myself as an indigenous Muslim American. But, anyway what she said to me I could identify with in part and appreciate it coming from her. She said, "I never thought of myself as African."

She said, "I never thought of myself as Black". She said,
"I accepted it because everybody else used it". She said, "I
never thought of myself as Black. I never thought of
myself as African." She said, "I always had a problem
with those kind of terms. I thought of myself as just an
American." She said, "I believe that we were the only
Americans and that everybody else were something else to
qualify themselves as Americans". She said, "like Italian
Americans, Jewish Americans, Spanish Americans." She
said, "What kind of Americans are we?" She said, "We
are just Americans!" Isn't that something? Yes! I
appreciate what she was saying. The people that came to
this part of the world, they saw it as a good prize for them
to capture. They came in as conquerors, and they
conquered this land and they took it. And they didn't give
up their identity.

They did not say, "Now and this day on we are
Americans". No! They said, "E Pluribus Unum A unity of
many." So, if you are Irish, you are still Irish, Irish
Americans. If you are Ghanain, you are still Ghanain
American, wherever you are from, you are still that, but
now you are in America. But, now look at us, in the

special kind of special situation that we have. This young girl said, "All the rest of them came to America". She said, "We did not come to America". Now, that is true too. For an overwhelming majority that is true. We did not come to America.

You know they ask you, "Where did you come from?" When they ask us that, we should say, "Anywhere"! They will say, "What do you mean?". Say. "I always have been here"! They will say, "No, you people came from Africa". Say, "No, we didn't come from Africa. They brought us from Africa!" So, people coming from some place, they prepare for the trip. So, those who came from those other nations, and other nationalities, and other lands, they prepared for the trip. They put in their traveling bag their past identity. But, we didn't come; we were brought. And we were brought suddenly. We were not allowed anytime to pack any bags.

You know the circumstances. So, we came here naked. And then they cut us off from any continuing communications with the land back there. So, we had nothing to live by except what we found in the circumstances that we were put in. So we can talk and talk and talk, philosophize and philosophize and philosophize, but we will come to a conclusion, if we have five good senses, that we are native Americans. What else are we? What else can we be other then native people of this soil? That is all that we can be, native people of this soil. I know they call the Indians the native Americans. But, they were not brought here. They came here. And they were not stripped. They had time to pack some bags and bring some identity from Asia with them. This is the history of the American Indians, that, they came from Asia by way of the Bering Straits. They came from Asia many, many thousands of years before the white man arrived. And they brought their culture with them to this part of the land. You who know the history, they brought their culture with them to this land. And there are students now studying the ruins and relics, ancient buildings on the first people called the Indians on this land. And many of them, in fact the majority of them have already come to the conclusion that they were once connected with Asian Culture and Asian life.

They found the same kind of structures, the same kind of culture in the Asian people's life. So, they have come to the conclusion that there must be a tie between, some of these native Indians that came here and African people, especially the Egyptians of northern Africa, they say the pyramids have too much of a resemblance for them to not have been somewhat connected in their past. So, we come to the conclusion that we are the only people of this soil. We are the only people that this soil has produced from the very beginning. What I mean, the beginning of our minds. All the other people came here with something already fixed into their minds. We came here with nothing fixed into our minds. And, those that had anything fixed into their minds, they wouldn't speak it for fear of death. And in time they died out. What they brought had no place in this part of the world because it was not allowed. That is the circumstances. But one day who knows, maybe we will ask them to recognize us as just Americans. And the rest of you are some kind of American.

We are just Americans, and who knows G-d may have a plan to give us the rule in this land. Who knows? "Aw, we are too weak. We don't have enough power. We don't have the numbers." Do you know how many people conquered Saudi Arabia and brought in the government? About 20! About 20 brave men following their brave leader, the late King Ibn Saud! The First king of Saudi Arabia, his name was Ibn Saud. And, he led a revolution to bring the people to respect the religion as it should be respected. They had started bringing in things in religion that was superstition.

Many of them had started to pray to ancestors. They would go to graves and pray for ancestors. Corruption was coming in Saudi Arabia where the Prophet (pbuh) established this great religion. And this great man, this great soldier for Allah, for G-d, Ibn Saud, he was a student of a School of Thought in Al-Islam called "Wahabism". And his teacher, Wahab, the man who headed that school Wahabism had excited his mind so much and made him so strong of a believer in G-d and Muhammad, the Prophet, (pbuh) and the follower of the Qur'an, that he couldn't tolerate any longer the corruption of the religion in Arabia.

It was not Saudi Arabia then, but because of his great victories, it was named for him, after Ibn Saud, Saudi Arabia. And right now if you go over there and see the Saudi Arabian people, they are a mixed up people like we are. Some of them look like white people. Some of them are black. But, the majority of them are brown people, where the majority of us are still black. The majority of them are brown people.

They have a few white looking people and a few very black people, and they are all Saudi Arabians. So, by the white man's description what are they? Are they black or white?

By the white man's terminology, by his language terminology, they are black people. Now, do you think that he will ever tell you Saudi Arabian people are black people. He will tell you that Ralph Bunche is a black man. And Ralph Bunche was as white as most Saudi Arabians. But, he will tell you Ralph Bunche is a black man, Dr. Ralph Bunche. You know who I am talking about. The one who went over into the middle east and made peace between the Jews and the Arabs. We need another Ralph Bunch to go over there with the Qur'an and try it again.

So, we must understand that Prophet Muhammad (pbuh) is the last messenger of G-d. And not the last, because we don't want to see another one following him, he is the last because G-d completed his favor upon us with Muhammad (pbuh). G-d completed what he wanted for the people on this earth with Muhammad of Arabia (pbuh). That is why he is the last. And whoever comes up with something now to advance the future for man or to improve the present or to explain the past, he can't come up with anything that hasn't already been given to Muhammad, the Prophet (pbuh). That is why you can't call another one a prophet. It doesn't mean that G-d won't reveal things to people. He will always reveal to people. It doesn't mean we won't have illuminated minds anymore. We will always have illuminated minds. But, we will never have anybody coming up with anything to add to what G-d gave as a plan for this whole world. So, in a scriptural sense, there are no more men or messengers coming from G-d. He is the last.

And again, I repeat, whatever we come up with, it has already been revealed. Well that is a enough for that. Praise be to Allah. Now, was the world expecting this man, this prophet? Yes! The world was expecting him. The religious world, the people who received the scriptures from messengers that came in the line of the progressions of prophets before him, Yes, they knew he was coming. They expected him. Many Jews, many Christians who heard Muhammad, the Prophet, pbuh, many of them who heard him in the time he preached in Arabia, they recognized him with tears flowing down their cheeks. They said, "This is the one that our scriptures told us about". And they became Muslims. They left their Judaism. They left their Christianity. And, they became Muslims.

You know that is what we fail to understand, I mean the western mind that looked at the Muslim World, failed to understand that Muhammad (pbuh) didn't convert people that didn't have religion. Where did he get the people from that is following him? He got them from persuasions that were existing when he was here on this earth bodily. He got them from the persuasions that were existing then,

Christian persuasions, Jewish persuasions. And also a kind of nature belief that most of his people in Arabia had.

They were naturalist who believed only in nature and that gods were only concepts or depictions, pictures made depictions of facets of nature, forces and facets of nature. But that wasn't only true for them. That is true for most of the ancient world. Most of the ancient world did the same thing. They followed nature until they saw nature guiding them to natures Lord. Nature has a Lord too. And when they found nature guiding them to nature's Lord, then they said, "Aw, this is the Lord of us all." And then they took the one Lord for their Lord. And this is given to us in the Qur'an; don't think that I am giving you anything that is not in the Qur'an.

This is given to us in the Qur'an, but not in the language that I put it. Those were my words but the same light is given to us in the Qur'an only much better. Now, dear people, so since they had some knowledge of this one coming, let us see what Allah told Muhammad (pbuh) of this in the Qur'an to let them know that this is the one that

G-d promised. I should begin with the prayer of Moses praying that G-d would stay with the people after he had passed. And Moses prayed, and now I quote what is given to you in the Qur'an what he said. "And ordain for us that which is good in this life and in the hereafter. For, we have turned unto thee." And G-d replied unto Moses and said, "with my punishment, I visit whom I will. But My mercy extendeth to all things. That mercy, I shall ordain it for those who do right and practice regular charity and those who believe in our signs" and the 157 verse follows that verse continuing the description of Muhammad, the Prophet (pbuh) in scripture. "Those who follow the Messenger, the unlettered Prophet, whom they find mentioned in their own scriptures, in the law and in the gospel, for he commands them what is just and forbids them what is evil, he allows them as lawful what is good and pure and he prohibits them from what is bad and impure. He frees them from their heavy burden and from the yolks that is upon them."

Isn't that the Liberator? That is the one with the moral excellence that makes him fit to liberate the whole society of man on earth. "So, it is those who believe in him, that honor him, help him and follow the light which is sent down with him." And follow the light which is sent down with him." So, what are we really following when we follow Muhammad (pbuh)? We are following G-d's guidance. For Muhammad (pbuh), without G-d's guidance, is not the man for us to follow. Muhammad (pbuh) with G-d-s guidance is the man for us to follow. And he earned the office because of obedience to his best impulses in his nature. For G-d says of him is this Holy book, "He has already lived a lifetime among you. Meaning, that they could not find no spot or blemish in him even before he received revelation. Forty years is very significant number. "So, it is those who believe in him that honor him, help him and follow the light that is sent down with him, it they who will prosper". G-d says, "It is those who will prosper."

Should we expect individual or nations to prosper for long, if they don't follow this? No! No! They will prosper for a little while. And as G-d says in the scriptures, the Bible and also this Holy Book, the Qur'an that their day of merry making is a defeat. They are fooled by it. They think that they are prospering when they are fastly moving toward their doom.

For now, about ten years almost, I have felt the presence of a deathly silence on the greatness of America. And, I don't feel it lifted yet. My soul feels it. Allah is my witness. G-d is my witness. Deep in my soul, I feel a judgment of G-d on the productivity of America. And, I have been feeling it now for about ten years. I don't feel that it has lifted. Now, with that observed or noted that Muhammad (pbuh) is the cause of necessity, the last prophet. Muhammad (pbuh), because of Divine Decree, is the last prophet. And he is not a prophet to some people, but to all people on this earth. And he is not a prophet from the elite, but a prophet from the common masses. Because the people, he himself is associated with or identified with taking on the same name that G-d gave him, which mean unschooled. He is called the ummiyee which mean for one person unschooled, uneducated, unlearned. And the people that he is associated with are called the ummiyun which means plural, the uneducated, the unschooled people. So, he is called an unschooled prophet raised up among the unschooled people to be a messenger to all people. That too is in fulfillment of scripture. For, scriptures says, in so many ways it says, "out of the mouth of babes should come perfect praise."

Babes means babes in knowledge, those who are not educated. "Out of the mouth of babes shall come perfect praise." So what is the perfect praise? The Qur'an! It begins with, Al hamdu lilahi rabbil alimeen, All praise is due to G-d, the Lord of all worlds. It begins with that perfect praise. If I say All praise to the Lord of Israel, that is not the perfect praise. That is imperfect. If I say All praise is due to the Lord of the Muslims, that is imperfect. Or, the lord of the Christians, that is imperfect. Until we give the right qualifications to the Lord, that He is Lord of all worlds, then if that be my lord, then all praises due to my Lord. And, that is the perfect praise. Say, "Out of the mouth of babes shall come perfect praise" but it doesn't only mean verbal testimony.

It means that their life, their behavior will be a reflection of what G-d had intended or what G-d had revealed. And therefore their life would be a testimony to the perfect guidance of G-d. We saw that on this earth in Muhammad, pbuh, and in his great companions who followed him, may G-d be pleased with them and on the great defenders of that way of life who succeeded them and remained for centuries following the religion as it should be followed. We saw that upon this earth. It was lost because, as Muhammad (pbuh) predicted; that his people would go to sleep in comforts and a materialist power would rise up and plague the life of not only them but the whole world. Prophet Muhammad (pbuh)predicted this.

He called that materialistic power the "Dajjal" who would be riding a donkey. The donkey is symbolic of the ignorant, undisciplined masses. See a donkey is hard to discipline. He rebels against discipline. He has a big head relative to the size of his body. And, huge ears. Hhe is always listening. Isn't that the donkey people, the donkey masses. Oh, that is a big description of the donkey masses. Oh, they are always listening. They want to hear everything that you say. But, when you start saying, "Ok, now you heard what I have to say, now can we sign your name up, you are going to follow this?" "Well, why do I have to follow that? I am a person, I am a man just like you."

Big ears, big old head, he has a whole lot to say. He can talk forever. When he runs out, he holds you with signals that will excite your expectations. He doesn't have anything to say, he says something to just hold you again. "Do you know who won the pennant in 1925; if there was a pennant in 1925?" He will say anything just to hold your attention. He has to keep talking. He has a lot to say. But, he is not ready to follow anything. Incorrigible masses rebel against discipline. Says, "that Dijjal will be riding them." Tell me, who did the Bolsheviks build their world on? The ignorant masses! Who have the Democrats rode upon? The ignorant masses! I blame them for the state of our people right now. Yes, I do! I blame the Communists and the Democrats for the state of the African-American people, the communists for their hidden devilishment, the Democrats for their powerful deceits.

Say, "What about the Republicans?" Well, they need to be condemned for their sins too! But, I am telling you the

Democrats want us to forget that it was a Republican that started the freedom process for the African-American man, indigenous African-American man. Yes, Abraham Lincoln was a Republican. The Democrats were racists! Isn't that a fact of history? The democrats were racists! How quick we forget! I am not saying the Republicans hasn't got their racists too. They got their racists. And they are a kind of Ivory tower boys, bankers and big shots. It is kind of hard for us to identify with them unless we come in as a servant.

I don't want to identify with them. I want to challenge them all. Yes, as an American, Muslim American challenge all of them. And again, G-d says in this Holy Book. "That Muhammad, the promised one, sent to the unlettered people or unschooled people to teach them the book and the wisdom and to purify them."

And to purify them, so let us give our attention for a few minutes to the need for purification, the need for purification in our lives or in the society. "He was sent to give them the book," the source of light and understanding, the highest source of light and understanding. That, that makes possible the development or the creation of all the other forms of knowledge that we need to live the full life on this earth. He was sent with that to teach them the book and the wisdom. Now, he is coming to a people that are unschooled.

If they are unschooled, even though they have government, they are in a high risk situation. Because, the learned nation will come against them and defeat them easily. Now, it doesn't mean that none of these uneducated people were not in power in the time of Muhammad (pbuh). Don't you know we've got many unlearned nations right now in power. Yes! In fact, most of the nations in the third world are unlearned. That is why they are the third world. That is why they are the situation that they are in. Because, as governments, they are not yet learned. So, the Prophet comes to a people like that. And that is in the Bible, that is in scriptures that came before. Understand this! Jesus is a great sign.

Christians know it, I mean learned Christians, the leaders
in Christianity. They know it. They know that Jesus is not
to really be seen, to be appreciated in the body like ours.
They know that Jesus is to be appreciated as a sign, not as
a body like this, no man like this. No! Only as a sign, that
is where he is really appreciated. So, Jesus came as a sign
or a depiction of the revelatory process; how G-d brought
revelation into the world through man. He is a sign of
many things. But more than anything else, he is a sign of
this. And this is given in the Bible in these words, "In the
beginning was the word and the word took on flesh,"
meaning in the beginning, there was the word of G-d in
revelation and the revelation in Jesus took on flesh. And
many understand it to mean, took on the problems of sin in
the world, that is true too. But, more than that, took on
flesh, meaning the word is depicted as flesh and dwelled
among men. So, this is the Bible. And G-d gives us the
light of understanding on this in the words of the Qur'an
that says, "That it is not G-d's desire or wish to put you
into any difficulties. But, it is His wish to purify you and
to perfect his blessings on you.

And we know that the same kind of language is given in that verse in that Qur'an of this Holy Book regarding the completion, the finishing of the revelation to Muhammad (pbuh), "This Day have I perfected for you your religion." Same language, same words, "and completed my favor on you, and I prefer for you Al-Islam the religion." This is the Qur'an, same words. So, it continues here, says "and that he may perfect his blessings on you."

Now, this same expression, "perfect his blessings on you" is given again in the Qur'an in this way, "that He may perfect His word." His word. So, His word is what he perfected. And in perfecting his word, he perfects his blessings and makes possible the completion of the message, the completion of the religion. So, the Christians says it in one way with Jesus Christ as a symbol for something greater behind the symbol or to be interpreted out of the symbol. And Allah says to us in the Qur'an in a plain language. And understand that our Holy Book says the same thing of Jesus, that he is a sign. In fact, it says he and his mother are signs.

So, let us continue on purity now, we are talking on purity. And I hope you are not in a hurry. It won't be too long. G-d willing, it won't be too long now. So, it says again, "Surely, Allah wants to take away from you corruption O people of the house, and to purify you for a lasting purity." Isn't that wonderful?! Now this was said to Muhammad, the Prophet (pbuh), revealed to him by G-d to be said directly to those people is his family, who lived in his own house.

Now maybe if Abdus Salaam was here today who is a Moroccan Muslim and a teacher here in our Schools, if he was here today, I am sure he would have difficulty accepting what I am going to say now, because there are those who understand in the Islamic world that "ahlil bait" is talking about the family of Muhammad. But, I believe that "Ahlil bait" is talking directly about the family of Muhammad (pbuh) but it includes all people who follow the religion strictly. All people who follow the religion strictly!

All Muslims who follow the religion strictly with a sense of obligation that the family of the Prophet had, all of us who carry that religion with that same sense of obligation are "Ahlil Bait." That is my belief. But, however they may differ with that. They have the Shiites that would differ with them even more then I differ with them. So, don't throw me out because I differ. Or say, "w0ho is he; where did he get his knowledge?" Well, let's talk to the intelligent audience and let the intelligent audience be the judge. I am ready anytime. Yes, so I believe this "ahlil baat" goes for all of us who follow the religion with the same conscious devotion that was established in the great relatives or the family of the Prophet.

And mind you, this was told to them because some of them had become a grievance, an annoyance to the Prophet, in his own family, because of their failure to live up to the highest standards for the Muslim society. And understand this also, that just as Muhammad (pbuh) had to be protected in his family, if we have great leaders today, we need protection in their family. So, anytime you see members of my family failing the standards, you should be concerned.

You shouldn't say, "Hey, look at his own children, hah, hah, hah." You should be hurt in your heart. They say, "Oh, look at his own house, look at the Imam's own family, hah, hah, hah." You shouldn't be like that! That is the enemy. That is the hypocrite. That is the infiltrator. You should be hurt in your heart and you should love the family of the Imam even though they deviate, because, all of us can deviate. And, you should have a desire in your heart to see them improve their conduct, not only for their benefit, but for the benefit of the need of an example in the house of our leader.

That was needed for the Prophet, it is need for all of our leaders, not just for me, for all of our leaders, even for the non-Muslim leader. Before, you pick a non-Muslim leader to be Mayor or Governor, or whatever, Attorney General, learn something about how he lives privately. And see if you find his house all messed up, see if his house is a rebel house or is he the leader. If, he is the leader or an associate, reject him. But, if his house is a rebel house, then let you heart go out to him and to his house. Yes!

They say, "Why should our heart go out to his house?"
Because, you need him and he needs his house! See, we
need to get bigger in our minds and hearts then what we
are. Then, we become a bigger people.

Concerning the Blessed Mother of Jesus (upon Him be
peace) and upon Her, G-d say's in the 'Quran' "Surely G-d
chose you." That is Mary, the Mother of Jesus "and
Purified You, and chose you to be above all the Women of
the World," Why did He choose Mary to be above all the
Women of the World? Because of Her Guaranteed
verified Purity.

The Prophet comes now to the Muslims, or to the World,
and He invites them to become Muslims. And to the
Muslims He was instructed to say to them, "You are the
best Community, brought out of the world, for the benefit
of all People." This is what G-d says of our Muslim
Community. The International Muslim Community, in
this Holy Book. And what else does He say? "You invite
to all that is good, and you prohibit all that is bad." And in
another place, G-d says to Mohammed, "Oh Mohammed,

tax their wealth, as a means of Purifying them". And then He say's of Mohammed, "That you are sent to teach them the Book, and the Wisdom, and to Purify them." And He says again to Mohammed, "It is not G-d's wish to put you into any difficulty, but it is His wish to make you Pure, to Purify you". So if Mary was a Sign, what is She a Sign of. She's a Sign of the Ummah. 'She's a Sign of the Islamic Community', established by Mohammed the Prophet (pbuh). Yes.

Now, many of us don't know that Mary was also a Sign of something to come. We know that Christ has to come again, because The Gospel says it. But many don't know that Mary is a Sign also of something to come. Not that Christ Himself would come, no, but what He represented with His Sign, would come. That that is not fulfilled, while He was here, because the Bible says the same. It was not fulfilled while He was here. Says "that when the Comforter comes, He would lead you into all Truths", and He didn't say, 'Thy Kingdom is Here.'

He said "Thy Kingdom Come." Now, many of us missed a little quiet signal in the Gospel. According to the future, also for His Mother. The Christian's give the incorrect picture of Jesus on the cross dying. The Qur'an gives the right picture, and He speaks in His death, which is not really His death. That's also a cloud, covering something else. He speaks out of the Gospel, and He says, "Look to your Mother". Look to your Mother is just like saying, "Look to the future.". But look to the future by what means, or through what focus, or window? He says, "Look to your Mother". So when Jesus was up on the Cross, He didn't say look for me.

According to the Gospel, He said, "Look to your Mother", because you won't see Him before you see your Mother. You following? Praise be to Allah. You won't see Him before you see your Mother. Now, I'm saying that the real Community of the Muslims (that was established by Mohammed The Prophet Himself) pbuh, is the fulfillment of the Sign of Mary, and Mohammed Himself, is the fulfillment of The Sign of Jesus. Oh!, but He was Father of our Community. No He wasn't! He said, "I am not the Father of any of your Children".

That's what Mohammed said, according to the Words of
G-d in His Quran. It says, "Oh Mohammed, I'm not the
Father of any of your Children." And He didn't teach
anybody to call Him Father like (The Christian Leaders
do). He said, "call each other Brother." They called Him
Mohammed, and they called Him Brother, not Father.
Messenger of G-d, Mohammed, and Brother. Oh, how can
that be explained now. How is He coming out of His
Mother. "And we raised up from among the illiterates."
He was raised up from among the illiterates. So what did
He come out of. He came out of the Ignorant People. And
the ignorant people He came out of are people who follow
nature but have not been made pure, until the blessing of
the coming of The Quran. With the Blessing of the Quran
they were purified. And Allah say's in the Quran, of
Mary, "And He Purified Her."

The Prophet said, "Surely Purity is the Seashore of Faith".
And they translated it, "Surely, Purity is half the Faith".
But when you come out of the water, upon the bank, the
bank should be the bank of Purity. And as you proceed on

into the land, going over the clean sands of the River, or the bank, you go into that land that will permit Harvest Production, planting, and harvest or production. But the water, then the clean sand, then the fertile soil, as you come out of the water. So that's why the Prophet has said, "Surely, Purity is the Seashore, or the bank of the Sea for the Faith, for Iman." If you're gonna be trusted. If you're gonna be trustworthy, and be trusted, then you have to have a preference in your life, and that preference should be for Moral Decency. And if it's not there, then we can't expect the Great Blessing of G-d. I conclude that on Purity now, and if you don't mind, I would like for you to be here just for a little while longer.

Returning to our theme on Joseph as a Sign, Allah says in His Holy Book, (the chapter is Joseph, Yusef) which is Joseph in English. Section 6, 43 verse.

The King of Egypt said, "I perceived in a vision 7 fat kines, whom 7 lean ones devoured, and 7 green ears of corn, and 7 others withered." Now the kine is spelled here, KINE, and it means, a young Cow. Then he saw in a

dream, 7 fat young calf's, and in the same dream, he saw 7
other calf's, that were very lean, and they were given to
devouring, or the 7 lean ones were the cause of the fat ones
being lost or eaten up. And 7 green ears of corn, and the 7
others withered.. "O you Chief's. Expound to me my
vision if it be that you can interpret visions." They said,
(Now here is the King of Egypt, He's talking to his
Learned Priest's, who are schooled in Interpretation, of
Highly Spiritual, or Psychological Matters). They said, "A
confused medley of Dreams, and we are not skilled in the
Interpretation of Dreams". So they said, "that this, what
you report O King, is confusion to us. Just a lot of
confusion to us. Just mixed confusion on top of confusion,
and we are not very skilled, we are not really skilled in
Interpretation of Dreams."

Just like those people that profess to be experts. They
profess Professionalism, but when you really got
something they can't handle, then they start talking about,
"Well in that particular area now, I'm not really
professional in that particular area. I think you should see
some specialist, a specialist for that particular area." But
as long as you don't catch them in a situation like that, oh,

they make you think they can handle everything. But the man who had been released, (one of the two who had been in prison) and who now be sought him after so long, (that is, remember Joseph).

You recall that Joseph told them after helping the two in prison). He was in prison, and they were in prison with him. (Joseph still in prison now, here in this reading). He told them, "Now remember me to your Lord when you get out". And your Lord then is like the Lord of London, or your Boss, you see. Your Big Chief. But they forgot. They got out and they were so happy over their freedom, they forgot. So now He remembered. (One of them remembered now when the King is in this difficulty).

He said, " I will tell you the Truth of its interpretation. send you me therefore." So He was sent, he was allowed to be sent to Joseph. He left, and he went to Joseph. " Oh Joseph," he said, "O man of Truth". " Expound to us the Dream of 7 fat Kine's, or Calf's, whom 7 lean one's devoured, and 7 green ears of corn, and 7 others withered, that I may return to the people, and that they may understand". Joseph said, " for 7 year's shall you diligently sow grain, (the seed's for crop), as is your want. And the harvest that you reap, you shall leave them in the ear except a little of which you shall eat". (He is telling them that when they sow, and the crop comes, to not eat freely, but to take a little.

Just enough to manage. Just enough, and leave most". Then will come after that a period of 7 dreadful year's, which will devour what you have laid by in advance for them. So He's telling them that G-d is going to bring, or they're gonna have 7 bad year's for their productivity, and that they should prepare for those 7 bad year's by saving much during the 7 good year's which you should have specially guarded. "Now, then will come after that, a year in which the people will have abundant water, and in which they will press wine and oil".

So the King says, " Bring you Him unto Me". (for when the messenger came to Him) Joseph said, "Go thy back to thy Lord and ask Him what is the state of Mind of the Ladies who cut their hands." Now Joseph was put in prison because the ladies, the leading ladies of Egypt had wanted to seduce him like the big lady did, but they were so excited over his beauty, his appearance, they cut their hand's. And when it was asked, " What happened here", Joseph was charged with cutting their hands" So he was charged with trying to seduce the Big Lady, and that was explained, and He was cleared of that, but when the little ladies came, they inflicted themselves, and caused bleeding from their hand's themselves, but Joseph had to bear the consequences, had to bear the burden of that, and he was put in jail. After all the other bad circumstances he had. So he wants this cleared up.

He says, "Ok, the King needs me now to interpret the dream for him, and they want to bring me there to help him. First clear my situation here. What about those ladies that charged me." So the King said to the ladies, "what was your affair when you did seek to seduce Joseph from his true self." The ladies said, "G-d preserve us." "No evil know we against Him" said Aziz's wife. The big lady said that. "no evil we know against him". Now, is the truth manifest to all. "It was I who sought to seduce him from his true self; he is indeed of those who are ever true and virtuous." So she admitted. the big lady admitted that she was the cause of it all. She started the whole thing. That she was the one. He had not done any wrong. That he has ever been true. That he is a man that is always true and virtuous.

"This say I, in order that He may know that I have never been false to Him in His absence:, She's telling Joseph that I haven't been false to You in your absence. That's what she wanted to tell Joseph. Now, you know the charges she made against Joseph, she made it in Joseph's face, didn't she. Yes, so she was false alright. She was wrong, but she didn't do it behind Joseph's back. She made a charge right in Joseph's face. She told a lie on Joseph right in his face to the King.

So she just wanted Him to know that I get you in trouble, but I don't do it to you behind your back. Isn't that something. It's all right isn't it. I hope you all can see deeper than the letters here on the page. You know, now this woman, she's cleaning up for herself, isn't she. I'm not saying she's Satan, but didn't Satan clean up for himself too. He said, " I didn't have any part in this". He said. " I didn't force anybody to do this". He said, "I invited them to do these thing. They came on their own. They shouldn't blame me. They should blame themselves, for making me their choice." So, he cleaned up too, didn't he?

But G-d says, "Hell is a fit place for you both; for you and your followers." That's Satan. See, that's why our religion is so great. When I was a child, I thought the devil (in Christianity), was an indestructible being. " You do that, the devil is going get you. You'll go to hell and burn forever." "The devil's going put you in the fire." I say, where is the devil? He's in hell". I say, " how in the hell can he live in hell with all that fire and do a job." But our Holy Book tells us differently. "Hell is not a comfortable place for even the devil". G-d says, "His punishment shall be that He shall be put in Hell too." Say's that, "and the fire there break's up men and stone." This I say in order that he may know that I have never been false to him in his absence, and that G-d will never guide the snare of the false one. Nor do I absorb my own-self of blame.

Now, she said, "I have to take some part of the blame now. I didn't do anything behind your back. By me saying this, don't think I'm saying that I'm not responsible for some wrong. I don't clear myself of all the blame now, she said." Look where she puts the blame though. She says, "The human soul is surely prone to evil." She blames her soul. It's the weakness of the soul, it is prone to evil. Unless my Lord do bestow his mercy. For surely my Lord is oft Forgiving, Most Merciful." This is wonderful.

The soul that is prone to evil. La-Amara means La. It is an intensifier in Arabic Grammar. La means that whatever is there, is compounded. It's made stronger, it's excessive. La-Amara if it's Amara and you put La before it, to make it La-Amara mean's it's compounded, it's intensified, it's excessive. Now, when we give ourselves to any desire, that it becomes an obsession, (wasn't she obsessed with getting Joseph), so it became an obsession for her. And what Allah is saying in the Quran, is that "The soul under the pressure of an obsession is inclined to do wrong." Now, when a Leader, (campaigning for positions of power and authority), if he allows the office that he is aspiring to, to become an obsession, Look Out! He might have been clean before, corruption most likely will set in. Right? So this is what Allah is saying. And some Muslims have made the mistake of thinking that what G-d is saying here, is that the human soul have a natural tendency to commit sin. That's wrong. You don't have a natural tendency to commit sin in your soul. You have a natural tendency to be right in your soul. It's when you start rationalizing, with your own small mind, right and wrong, the benefits, and the consequences. When you let your own little small knowledge come into the picture, that's when you start to commit great sin. No baby comes here committing any great sin. The baby comes here trying to go right. And they remain decent and nice, until they get into this mind that they can make decisions for themselves; start trusting their own limited minds.

This is where we differ so much with Christianity, and many other religions. They say "the flesh is weak. The spirit is willing, (I think, is that the way it goes) but the flesh is weak." We don't have that kind of idea. We reject that. That's wrong. Flesh is strong. The mind is given to be weak in bad circumstances. The flesh is strong. Flesh is strong. Nature is strong. Spirit is strong, when that spirit is in agreement with the excellence of nature. Nature is born like a worm that has to grow into special form. There is a silk worm, that come as a worm. But there are other worms that come as a worm, but they have a metamorphosis. They rise from a worm to an elaborate creature.

Well symbolically speaking, in our nature, we're like a worm that has to come to a metamorphosis. A transition. A trigger or a gear into higher elevation. The apparatus for this transition is also a property of that nature, in the word, so the nature has in it already, a program for advancing the quality of the creature. He may be born in a shallow place, in a filthy place, in a dark dismal place, in swamp water, in all kinds of slimy stuff, but there is a program in him, that nature has put in him, that programs him to come up the scale of evolution. We don't judge nature, by what she is in her embryonic stage unless we can see into her embryonic stage, her mighty program, for the future. So let's not be like the rest of the world and think that flesh of man is weak, and prone to sin. But let us think as G-d want us to think in this religion, and this Quran.

Let us think that G-d has made the nature of man excellent, and his flesh is obedient to G-d. Do you know Prophet Mohammed (pbuh) only stood for a dead body. He never stood for a living body when a man was in it, responsible for his behavior. But when there was funeral, and a body was dead, if Prophet Mohammed,(pbuh) was sitting, when He saw the procession coming by he would stand. Why? What was the wisdom he was giving? He was given in that demonstration. He was saying as a testimony from himself, "G-d, I recognize the flesh that you made to be excellent, worthy of respect, and the wrong is not the flesh, but the ignorant creature that was responsible for the flesh while he lived, or while she lived". So we should understand that.

So she blamed it on the soul. Isn't that the same thing the West does. "Well, you know only G-d is divine. The human being is weak and prone to error. After all, he is only human." That's their language. "Excuse him because the soul is given to sin unless you confess the lord Jesus Christ and be born again." And be born again. Not

human, but be born thru his divinity. Be saved by his
divinity.

What they look at in Jesus, as his divinity. We see it as his
nature. We see it also as our nature. It's not divine, it's not
G-d, it's human nature. To be obedient to G-d. To care
about the suffering. To accept death, rather than give in to
the sinners. Whatever he has done, was nothing but
human. What they call his divine excellence is really our
excellence, and they call being born again thru Jesus, is
nothing but being born again thru a rejuvenation of your
own moral nature. See our religion respects what is right
and proper, and does not cloud the picture with a whole lot
of esoterics.

So, the King said, "Bring him unto me. I will take him
specially to serve about my own person." Therefore, when
he had spoken to him, he said "be assured this day, thou art
before our own presence with rank firmly established."
Didn't G-d say that he established Joseph in the land. So,
the King said, "be assured that you are with rank, firmly
established, and fidelity fully proved" (meaning that his

trust worthiness, his honor, his integrity, had been fully proved).

Joseph said, " Set me now, over the storehouses of the land. I will indeed guard them." Now, this is the story of Joseph. What you must understand that in the Story of Joseph, G-d says, " In the story of Joseph is a great sign to all the seekers." So Joseph said, "now set me over the store houses." So who should we put in, over the distribution of goods, over the regulation of affairs, the regulation of the distribution of wealth. All governments must have some regulations. Who should we entrust to be over that? To be fair and just by all people. Someone who's integrity has been proven beyond a shadow of a doubt. Someone who has been tested, and passed the test. Who came under the great pressure, who came under the great test, and passed the test. Not only as an individual, but as a people.

For G-d tests persons, and He tests people. And we were on the way to come into the position of Joseph, but we let the turbulent sixties, and all of its deceits, (the invitation to get the green dollar), the high emphasis on black beauty, and black power. We let all those deceits, and the invitation to smoke reefers, and burn incense, and go backwards in the path of civilization, rather than forward. To go to crime, and oppress your own weak people. Black on black crime. All of that mess that developed, knocked us out of the great opportunity to become the Joseph of the Western Hemisphere. Why, if we had been loyal to our profession, to our professions, to our claims, if we had been loyal to our better aspirations as we published all over the this land, and throughout the world. If we had remained loyal as a people to those high aspirations, today, we would be the most beloved people in the Western hemisphere. And people that's before us, in position of risks of high end to the other people.

Because we were people, and our forefathers, and our ancestors, following the spirit of freedom, the spirit of high moral conscious, high moral minds, the spirit of obedience to G-d that was all together with us. And we were warning the racist, warning the white man, that if he didn't hurry up and do what G-d wants, that G-d would bring terrible consequences on him. And if he is a conscious Christian, he should see his sins and repent. Wasn't that the voice of the African American (Indigenous African American) until he got freedom. Then when he got freedom, He forgot. And as a consequence, he knocked himself out of the opportunity to become Joseph of the land. Who Knows, maybe we succeeded? Maybe Joseph is right here? Who knows? Yes, who knows? Maybe in this small community of Muslims, maybe we are the Joseph? Now, I know we got a lot of bull out there too, but I'm talking about the good ones. I didn't invite the bull. I am not responsible for their presence here. But those who are truly and sincerely behind what I represent as a Muslim, maybe we are the Joseph. I think we have passed the test.

He say's "set me over the storehouse. I will indeed guard them as one that knows their importance." Isn't that wonderful. He would guard them as one that knows their importance. So Joseph was a morally oriented or a disciplined man before G-d established him. Because of him being a morally disciplined man, G-d chose him to establish him. But G-d said that He was going to teach him the interpretation of things that had been recorded or reported, and try him in situations in order to establish him in the land. He had the moral quality, and the moral tenacity, the obedience to his moral excellence. He had that, but G-d wanted to make him fit for the position over the man. To make him fit, G-d had to put him through trials so the world, looking on, would know that He has been qualified. Yes. They put him in all kinds of situations under the most powerful, and under the most wicked, and brought him through. Proved his excellence in all of those trying situations, G-d proved His excellence. And He taught him the Secret of things. The mystery of things to be interpreted. And He said, "in that wise, we establish Joseph in the land". The Bible says, "thus did we give established power to Joseph in the land to take possession therein." Didn't G-d say in the scripture, "My righteous servant shall inherit the land. The wicked shall not rule continually." G-d said, "H\he shall lead them on by their deceit to their doom." And He said, "my righteous servant shall inherit the land."

We have forgotten that. I'm not talking about we, the public. I'm talking about we, the religious establishment. We have forgotten that G-d has required righteousness of us, in order for us to be put over the wicked, for if we don't have righteousness and only have the claim of being religious people, that doesn't give G-d the justice to put us over them. Only when we're righteous, and they're wicked. We're obedient to the moral code, to the moral law, and they're disobedient. They disrespect it. Then G-d will choose the righteous over the wicked. Is that clear as day?

So don't think that G-d calls us to be clean and Saintly, and holy for an inferior role on this earth. He calls us to be excellent in every respect and it begins with moral obedience. Not for an inferior role on this earth, but for the choicest role on this earth. And there will come to past, over and over again, and still the people fail to see that it is the righteous that G-d gives the power too, and give the land too, if they will only stand up, and be what they're professing to be, therein for to take possession of the land therein.

We bestow of our Mercy on whom We please, and We suffer not to be lost any reward of those who do good. So if we remain constantly obedient to G-d it may be some time coming, but know for certain, that eventually, you will be put over your oppressors, your persecutors. Those who throw spiritual corruption in the path of your moral struggle. You will be put over them, and G-d will remove that headache from your life. It came with Mohammed, (pbuh). It came with righteous servants of G-d, before Mohammed (pbuh). It can come again if you all would only be strong. But G-d wants us to know that this great station on earth, that we can have, is not better than the hereafter. So, the next verse says, "But verily the reward of the hereafter is the best, for those who believe, and are constant in their righteousness." Praise be to Allah. So we go back to chapter 8 titled Joseph. We hope to continue it at another time. In it as G-d say's in His Holy Book, "Great signs for the seekers". And I hope we are putting the emphasis where they are, in this Holy Book and I hope we will, as a people, admire this excellence that G-d has created in the nature of man, as exemplified in the life of Joseph here in this chapter. Actually, the fulfillment of that Joseph, is again, Mohammed The Prophet, (pbuh). Yes! Mohammed The Prophet (pbuh). Because it was his moral excellence that made even the idolater's (before he was missioned as a prophet), trust him over the storehouses.

Yes! They would come to him as though he was a bank, and leave their possessions with him when they were traveling out of the country, out of the vicinity. Yes! And eventually, G-d put him over all of the storehouses, didn't He. Yes! So understand that really, Joseph was fulfilled in Mohammed (pbuh), but he's not only a sign, of what was fulfilled in Mohammed (pbuh), he's a sign to all people in an oppressed condition. (the pre-Islam day Arab's) were oppressed by their ignorance.

We have been oppressed by ignorance and also by racist powers, and oppressive powers. So people are oppressed in different ways. We haven't only had our moral life, and our intellect thrown into prison, or into the hole, behind bars. We have had our whole physical life contained in prison. In slavery, and in prison on plantations.

Don't you know the prison system right now is set up for the ignorant? And a lot of us that are in jail shouldn't be there, victims of circumstances. So let us understand this, and I conclude this now. I thank G-d for blessing us to be here today. This prayer in Arabic is a regular prayer said by Muslims offered, "O Lord, do not allow our hearts to go back to corruption after You guided us, and give us from Your presence, mercy". Ameen. Peace be unto you.

We never can take for granted that everyone here knows about our religion, or knows Al-Fatihah, or anything of our religion, of the Muslims. So we have to read, though for most of us it's not necessary to read English, we have to read the English for the benefit of those who don't know, or who are interested in knowing something about Muslim life, what they believe, etc, what we believe etc.

So I will read the translation given here by an international respected scholar, and he gives the English translation of the standard prayer of the Muslims. This prayer is called the most often repeated verses, seven versus in the Quran. And it is said, for all occasions; we cannot do any prayer of the five prayers, or the five formal prayers without giving this prayer in the beginning of it. It read's in English, "The Title, The Opening". The first verse reads " With G-d's Name, Most Gracious Most Merciful". The second verse, "Praise be to G-d, The Cherisher, and The Sustainer of The World's". The third Verse, "Most Gracious,. Most Merciful". The forth Verse, "Master of The Day of Judgment". The fifth verse " Thee do We Worship, and Thine Aide We Seek". The sixth Verse, "Show Us the Straight Way". And the seventh Verse, " The way of those on Whom Thou hast bestowed Thy Grace, Those Whose Portion is not Wrath, and who go not Astray". And as the English People say, Amen. In Arabic, the word is Ameen.

Some people seem hesitant to say Amen, but we are not hesitant to say The Beneficent, The Merciful. Why? The Beneficent, The Merciful is English. So, I just would like to make those comfortable who have really no problem in their hearts. No need of us being burdened for nothing. Burdened enough just to get up and wake up and open your eyes. That's burden enough.

We want to comment on the story of Joseph again. In the 12th Chapter of the Quran. The Quran is the Arabic term which can't be translated except in a way that is only an explanation of the name. There's no one name, for Quran so it's translated into English, (that which is to be recited, read and recited).

Before reading the Quran, we should ask G-d's protection, or refuge with Him from the rejected Satan. We don't have to say it aloud, we can say it within our own hearts, and then say, "With G-d's Name, Most Gracious, Most Compassionate, or The Beneficent, The Merciful". And then we begin reading from Quran.

"Bismillah Ir Rahman Ir Rahim. With G-d's Name, The Beneficent, The Merciful." Then came Joseph's brethren. They entered his presence and he knew them, but they knew him not. And when he had furnished them with provisions, suitable for them, he said, bring unto me, a brother you have of the same father as yourselves, but a different mother." See you not that I pay out full measure and that I do provide the best hospitality." Now, as we mentioned last time when we were discussing Joseph as a sign, for the secrets of understanding. We mentioned that

Joseph is the honest, G-d fearing person who obeys G-d in everything.

And he was such a person before G-d missioned him. And according to the Quran, (the Word of G-d to the Muslims) G-d was protecting him, even before he was given his mission. And he had to go through many trials, be put in terrible situations. Captivity, imprisonment, but G-d was always with him, and watching him, and overseeing, without his knowledge, his care.

We should understand then, by that, that if any human being will be honest and sincere, that human being will have that same closeness, that same protection from G-d. Any human being will make it their purpose, their greatest concern to be right, to not be wrong, G-d will be by them all the time. They won't have to worry. They may fall into bad circumstances like Joseph did, but the end will be good. As Joseph's end was very good. Here it is mentioned that Joseph was not the child of the same mother, as the other boy's, the other children, who conspired against him. They were of a different mother.

However, there was a young brother, younger than even Joseph, and the bible gives his name as Benjamin, who was Joseph's full brother. He was the son of Joseph's mother. They were sons or children of the same mother. And here the holy scripture is telling us that Joseph longed to have his full brother freed from those conspirators, who were sons by another mother but of the same father, Jacob and in Arabic, or in the language of Quran, he is called Yakub.

And the reading continues now "for if you bring him not to me, you should have no measure of corn from me, nor should you even come near me." This is his demand he makes; he puts them in a situation where they have to bring his younger brother by the same mother, his mother, in order to get provisions from Egypt. They sold (you will recall), those who were here, they sold Joseph in captivity, and he finally ended up in prison in Egypt. And because of his ability to analyze a person's situation, or problems, the news of his skill reached those who were over the prison, and the King himself had problems, so he wanted Joseph to come help him with his problems. So Joseph got free, and finally, the King gave Joseph the position of chief over the distribution of goods, or provisions. It was a time of great famine. It is believed that the known world at that time was experiencing starvation.

And Egypt had plenty, and G-d put Joseph into a very good situation there and he became the one who's in charge of allowing or not allowing provisions to be given to different people or different nations who were asking for assistance, or provisions. So the one that they esteemed to be worthless, because G-d mentioned in the Holy Book here, and you'll recall, G-d mentioned how they valued him to be so cheap. But G-d valued him because of his honesty, and his decency, to be high and esteemed. But they valued him to be so cheap, so worthless. The one that they valued to be worthless, turned out to be in charge of the storehouse, as it is called in scripture.

He put Joseph over the storehouse. So when Joseph (Yusef, his name in qur'an language) made this demand, they answered and said, "we shall certainly seek to get our wish about him from his father. Indeed we shall do it." So they didn't want to act on their own, they had to go back and see the old man, Jacob.

And we say, on him be peace, because this Yakub is not the Jacob of the Bible. The Jacob of the Quran, is a figure worthy of being a Prophet of G-d. And Joseph told his servants to put their stock and trade, with which they had bartered, into their saddle bags. So they should know it only when they return to their people; they thought they were going away empty handed. Joseph let them think that. But he had his assistant's put their stock and trade, (the things that they needed) inside their saddle bags. So, actually, they had gotten what they wanted, but they didn't know it. So they went home. They went back to their father, and they told their father of the man, and that they couldn't get provisions unless they bring back their younger brother, Benjamin.

And the old man, he said, "No! I trusted you with Joseph and look what his fate was." So he didn't want to trust them with Benjamin. Now when they returned to their father, they said, " Oh father, no more measure of grain shall we get, unless we take our brother. So send our brother with us that we may get our measure. And we will indeed take every care of him". And the Father said "shall I trust you with any results other than when I trusted you with his brother before. But G-d is the best to take care of him, and He is The Most Merciful of those to show mercy."

When they opened the baggage, they found their stock and trade had been returned to them. They said, " Oh, our father, what more can we desire. This, our stock and trade has been returned to us." And then they said, " so we shall get more food for our family. We shall take care of our brother, and add at the same time a full camel's load of grain to our provision. This is but a small quantity." Jacob said "never will I send him with you until you swear a solemn oath to me in G-d's name, that you'll be sure to bring him back to me, unless you are yourselves hemmed in and made powerless." And when they had sworn their solemn oath to Jacob that is, their father, He said, "Be G-d The Witness and Guardian." So He (Jacob) took their oath before G-d. The oath was taken before G-d. Further He said, "Oh my sons, enter not all by one gate. The word for gate is also translated door, Ba-bin which means gate or door, commonly door, called Ba-bin in Arabic. So enter not by one gate. However cities, the big gates of the cities are called gates in English, and not doors, the old fashioned city gates, "Enter you by different gates."

Not that I can profit you anything against G-d with my advice. If you don't know something about the previous scripture, the report that the Bible gives of Jacob, then you won't get all of this that's in this report of the Quran. It is clearing Jacob of the charges that he was a clever trickster. Another word, they called Him a supplanter. An underminer, who undermines establishments, or people; who turns things upside down. So here the Quran is addressing that. He gave his sons advice, but his advice that he gave them was a strategy for getting the best results. It doesn't mean that he was wicked because he was a strategist. So the Quran is saying Jacob was a strategist; he was not wicked. So men are allowed to use strategy. We don't have to reveal everything we are doing. We are allowed to use strategy as long as our strategy doesn't violate good principles. So that's what the Quran is saying. It's very important to know that, and the wisdom, "do not enter all by one gate."

We have talked on this before, but I'll mention it again because I think some of us, perhaps, did not hear that address. A people like ourselves, an unestablished people; a people who are not established. What do I mean establish? In a position where the society is dependent upon your vision, upon your intelligence, upon your decisions. America is not dependent upon our vision, our decisions, etc. etc.

Not even this little neighborhood over here depended upon our vision, our intelligence, or our decisions. Not even the block you're on is dependent upon our vision, our intelligence, our decisions. Others are taking care of all of that. We just live there. So, when a people in a situation like us, like we're in, you say "Oh, yes it is, Harold Washington, takes care of it". That's what you think. In fact, most of you know better. If he made decisions, things would change. I'm sure he's not satisfied with the way things are. But I hear he's coming up with a new energy plan. A new way to provide energy, gas to the City. At least they're thinking about it seriously. And it was after I cut off the gas here. I kind of believe all of those thousands of dollars they were charging us, illegally, was paying his salary maybe. Yeah, they were collection enough from us to take care of Mayor Washington..

It's a little cool in here, but isn't it nice. Oh, it feels so good to me. It never felt this nice in this place. Seventeen thousand dollars, staying in our hands, and pockets, and being applied to our needs, that's not going out to them every two or three months. In fact, every two months, running about eight thousand dollars a month, sometimes better. And I was told before I came in, as the leader here, it was running much higher than that; much higher. That's what I'm told. That's terrible. I don't see how they could stand it. It was enough to make me want to fight somebody. See, when I came in, other people were taking care of all these things. So I didn't bother. But as money became more and more scarce, then the people who were taking care of it, they had to bring it to me. And then, when I looked at it, I said, "Good G-d Almighty! We can't stand this, we can't take this situation." And we are not gonna take it. We're gonna do what is intelligent. What is intelligent and decent.

You just don't do that. You don't make poor people pay eight thousand dollars a month for some gas. Just to come here and have the facilities open to a prayer and lectures, that's ridiculous. So we're permitted to use strategy as long as we don't violate decent principles. And we are advised according to this Revelation. When you are on the outside, and you want to get into a society, or a people that are not you, and not like you, and don't believe in what you believe in, don't just try one door, to get into them, you have to try various doors. And the door is only symbolic of any heavenly way. Go by in any heavenly way, approved by G-d. Any way that is high, that is decent, that is above the vulgar kind of mind and thinking, and behavior. Try any honorable way, that's all it means. Try any honorable way.

So, some have to go in with business strategy, others have to go in with political strategy, and still others will go in with academic strategy. And others will go in with moral strategy, and some will go in with social strategy. There are many strategies. And we all in our own knowledge, and our own strength, if we use our intelligence and have a plan to go forward in a foreign society to our beliefs, we can make it.

Then if we can't make it, if you tried all of that and you can't make it, then you should either leave, give it up, go somewhere else, forget that place, because G-d says, "My earth is vast." And when Judgment Day comes, those who say, "O G-d, we wanted to live your Religion, but we had no freedom to live your Religion under these oppressors." G-d will say, "didn't you know my earth was spacious?" This is the word of G-d to us in the Quran. "Didn't you know my earth was spacious?" And Mohammed the Prophet (pbuh); when he was boycotted, persecuted, and the old people were suffering, and the young were suffering because of the harsh bad situations they were in... He was weak in numbers, very few people. He couldn't defeat that powerful, ignorant society. So what did He do? He migrated, he left it. He went to a place that was friendly, opened their arms to him.

He went to Medina, and there established the first organized system of Al-Islam. The first Muslim society. So we have not only the Word of G-d telling us to do that, we have Mohammed (pbuh), as an example doing that. Yes. But once there is a situation for you to exist and progress, then you shouldn't leave there. You shouldn't leave there.

The time for us to leave America, was one-hundred years ago; after we've made all this progress, to create a climate of respect, or at least acceptance on the pages of the book, (of law books), whether it's in the heart of every white man or not, it's on the law books. After we've made this much success, this much progress, then you're foolish to talk about going somewhere else, because we're not wanted here. Well, look at yourself and see if you're wanted in your own heart. A lot of us, if we really looked at ourselves, we wouldn't be wanted in our own hearts.

So let's make ourselves acceptable. And then tell the world we've made ourselves acceptable. Now, what's your excuse for not excepting us? Wouldn't that be more intelligent? Thank you for Light! I was thanking G-d. I just used that occasion to thank G-d for a brighter light, not that little bulb up there. So we shouldn't depend upon just one strategy. Do you know that the African American mass movement has depended upon one strategy? We're comparing; the purpose of this talk on Joseph is to compare Joseph's situation with our situation. When we were made slaves in this country, we had no one to call upon but G-d There was no friend around here to help us. We were under our slave masters on the plantation. No friends to help us.

The north ignored our situation, until they came the commercial movement in the United States, and they needed the factory labor and etc., for the commercial movement. And they wanted to take those slaves away from the agricultural movement and bring them to the commercial movement. Now, that's one explanation for the freedom of the slaves. There are many explanations why we were freed. One is, the good people that were allowed to think. See when there is a situation that won't allow good people to think, good people tolerate a lot of bad things. But when the situation comes that allow good

121

people to think clearly, then the pressure of good people bears on those who are responsible for the wrong. So that was a fact in our freedom. But there are many other factors, that it take scholars of history to find. And one of them is just what I said, "there was a big commercial movement going on from the people in the northeast, and they needed the slave labor to do the great work that they knew would be soon required."

so they needed you to come up north for factory work, away from the agricultural work on the plantation. That was one of the reasons. So they used their power to bring about a climate for clear thinking on the issue of slavery and because of that good circumstance, Fredrick Douglas was heard. Well, I didn't mean to digress, in fact, we didn't. We're talking on, we're trying to make a comparison between the two. So Joseph, like us... we had nobody to depend upon but G-d. Look at Joseph, all of his brothers. That means the whole society, that's what it means. His father was old, and his brothers was running things. His father wasn't running things. His father was complaining against their behavior, but his father didn't have the vigor, that he had when he was younger to go out and take charge of the matter himself. So the father was sitting back, almost helpless, and just saying, " well, G-d knows what you are doing. G-d knows what you boys are doing. You're going to have to answer for this. And I will never approve of what you're doing."

But the old man was in the kind of situation where he couldn't do much. So who was Joseph under? Really, in his society, he was under his brother. So actually, he was a victim of nothing but conspirators; the victim of nothing but conspirators. He had nobody to cry to but G-d, and they sold him to the enemy. And he cried to G-d. No, he didn't know how to cry to G-d. But G-d knew his situation, and G-d came to him without him even calling on G-d. And again, that compares, because we didn't know how to call on G-d.

When the white people bring you and put you in slavery, and then tell you the thunder of G-d is the one you should turn too, and gives you his image and his light, I'm telling you that's a problem. That's a problem for any intelligent slave. It isn't a problem for a brain washed slave, but it is a problem for any free thinking slave. Now you are the people that have mistreated me. You're the people that have called me sub-human and put me in this bad shape. Now you tell me one of your kind is my god . What kind of Trick is this? That's what a free thinking slave would be ready to sing. That's what he would be registering in his heart if he didn't have the courage to speak it. And you know, it's documented that some of our people registered that in their hearts, and they said it in a clever way where they couldn't be charged by the slave master.

Julia is a slave, it is documented that she commented on the cruelties of the white man to their slaves. And she said, "You people, you look like G-d in the face, but act like the devil in your hearts." So what was she saying to them? "I don't believe you, you're a liar. The white man is no G-d. Your face is a lie, your heart is a devil." That's what she was saying. So really I read that, and I said look, The Honorable Elijah Muhammad wasn't the first one to call white folks devils. Julia called them devils but in a clever way. Why? Because she said, "your heart is devil." She said, "you look like G-d in the face, but act like the devil in your heart."

So she said your heart is devil. According to the their Bible, the heart is a real problem. "As a man thinketh in his heart, so is he" that's the Bible. So, Julia called them the devil and she was right. And The Honorable Elijah Muhammad called them the devil, and he was right. It's just not to be taken literally like he told it. But He was right. Now, I can explain that more clearly for you at another time.

So you will say, "yes Brother Imam, he was right." You may say, "well isn't the black man the devil?" No, the black man isn't the devil. The black man may be a devil, but the black man is not the devil. He hasn't enough on the ball to be the devil. The devil has got power; the devil works great strategy; powerful deceiver. The Black Man just had about ten or twenty years of practice. Maybe forty years from now he'll be the devil if he's allowed the freedom, but he is not the devil yet. Keep looking to Farrakhan you may turn out to be the devil because he's well on the way to creating devils. Get you to double talking, doing wrong in the name of G-d. Pretty soon, you'll be the devil. "Oh! Why you attack Farrakhan?" Well, when he cleans himself up, I won't attack him. They tell me he's corrected his ways. If he's corrected his way's why doesn't he do what I did? Let it be known, people looking at me out in the street because they saw us on television. They think I got an apology? A woman looked at me like she wanted to spit on me. I looked back at her like I wanted to puke on her. And she just walked away. She couldn't stand my look, because she was guilty.

So you see what Allah says of Jacob in the Quran. It says, "he advised these conspirators, because his soul was burdened." As human beings, you know we would do all we can if we are motivated by good. We would do all we can to direct wrong people in the right way. So those were his children, and he was doing all he could for his children as an old man, with his heart going out to them. He knew they were conspirators. He knew they were wrong. But He gave them the right advise. But Allah says, "they could not benefit from the advise that their father gave them because it was not G-d's will to let wrong people benefit from the advise." And the Quran speaks highly of Jacob; say's 'He was full of knowledge and experience."

Now, when they came into Joseph's presence, he received his full brother to stay with him. He said to him, "behold, I am thy own brother. So grieve not at anything, of their doing." At length, when he had furnished them forth, with provisions, suitable for them, he put the drinking cup into his brothers saddle bags, then shouted out, "Oh you in the caravan." And those were his brothers, they had come with the caravan of camels, to get the provisions. "Oh you in the caravan, behold! You are thieves without doubt." Now Joseph himself, didn't make this shout. When he brought the attention to his security people, one of his security people cried out. It goes on to say, "they said, turning towards them, what is it that you miss?" And they said, the people on the other side with Joseph, "we miss the great beaker of the King". Now the beaker of the King is the cup. The King's cup. "For him who produces it, is the reward of a camel's load. I will be bound by the promise." That's what Joseph said to them.

The Brother said, "y G-d, you know well that we come not to make mischief in the land, and we're no thieves." The

Egyptians said, "what then should be the penalty of this, if you have proved to have lied?" They said, "the penalty shall be that he in whos saddle bag it is found, should be held as the bondsman to atone to repent for his wrong." Thus it is that we punish the wrong doers. So he began to search through their baggage. Before he came to the baggage of his brother, at length, he brought it out of his brother's bag. Joseph pretended like he was looking for it, and finally, he went to his brother's bag, and he brought it out of his brothers bag.

Thus did we plan for Joseph. He could not take his brother by law. There was no law in Egypt that would permit him to adopt his brother, or to have his brother come into his charge. So this was the way he got his brother. "We raised to degree's of wisdom, whom we please, but overall, endued with knowledge, is One, The All Knowing, That is G-d." They said, "if he steals, there was a brother of his, who did steal before him." But these things, did Joseph keep locked in his heart, revealing not the secrets of them. He simply said to himself, "you are the worst situated, and G-d knows best, the truth of what you assert." So Joseph was hearing what the Egyptians were saying, and he was saying that he wasn't going to speak out because actually, his situation was kind of precarious there too. He was not in a good situation, because if he showed any sign that he was differing with the Egyptians, then maybe he would be denied that favored position that he had been given. So he was very clever not to let everything be known of the situation. He was one gifted with the power of interpretation from G-d, because of his purity, because of his inner purity. He was gifted with the power of insight, and interpretation. So he knew the correct answer for those things that happened (or the correct explanation), but he refused to let it be known for fear that his situation would change with the Egyptians.

They said, "oh exalted one, behold. he has a father, aged and honorable who would grieve for him. So take one of us in his place, for we see that you are gracious in doing good." For they are pleading now because they fear what the old man is going to say to them when they get back. He'll say, "Oh yes, you took Joseph, now you've come back empty handed." "Where is Benjamin?" The Bible calls him Benjamin. They were worried about that, so now they're pleading to have the brother returned. He said (meaning Joseph), "G-d forbid that we take other than him with whom we found our property. Indeed, if we did so we should be acting wrongfully."

So let us make some comments, some closing comments on this section that we read, especially on the strategy of Joseph. You see, Joseph uses strategy. His father was a strategist. Now Joseph had been blessed with great knowledge and insight, but his situation is precarious, so he now uses strategy. He causes his brother to be suspected as a thief. But what is he stolen? He's stolen the cup of the King. Now, Joseph could have defended himself if they had really been in a situation when Joseph could make it known just what his situation was, and just what everything was all about. He could have defended himself. He could have said, " Well King, the cup you got is not for you only. The cup you got is for all G-d's people." The cup is a symbol. It has a symbolic meaning; the cup of the King means that knowledge of how to get pure understanding." The King had it, he had it just for himself. The knowledge to get clear and pure understanding, he just had it for himself. So actually, Joseph wasn't taking aothing that didn't belong to him, and everybody else. For he took the King's cup and put it into his brothers saddle bag. That's where it belongs. The cup belongs in his brothers saddle bags, because his brother was oppressed, denied freedom, etc. because he was persecuted (being a brother of that mother that Joseph was a Son to), he was persecuted by his brothers too.

He wasn't accepted among them. They didn't accept Benjamin among them, the younger brother. So His situation was bad too. And Joseph wanted to help his brother out. I got free, but now I want to help my brother His younger brother, who was in the same situation as a child of his same mother. So He had a strategy, he didn't do any wrong. He picked up the King's cup, the cup is not the Kings. The rights of this kind of knowledge that this cup is symbolic of, is every man's right. So he puts it into his brother's saddle bags. But now, his brother is suspected as being a thief.

Now, the King is not going to let him go away. "You can't go away, having this knowledge, young boy. You've got to stay with us now." And that's just what Joseph wanted.

He wanted them to hold his brother back so he and his brother could support each other. His brother had one principle of the human potential that was strong in him, and Joseph had the other twin principle that was strong in him, and Joseph wanted to bring the two principles close, so they could benefit from each other.

G-d has blessed me with a certain kind of insight, a certain kind of ability, and my youngest brother, He saved him for another kind of insight, another kind of ability. So I want him to be close to me and the two of us, together, we'll benefit each other, and give support to each other. And we should be together. G-d created us to be together. We are brothers by the same mother and by the same father, so that's symbolic. We're speaking symbolically, and trying to give some interpretation as we go.

So he devised a plan, or strategy, for getting his brother in Egypt with Him. And it worked. Now, when his brothers went back, they were in trouble, and so we will continue to read it later. But there is one verse that we want to make some comment on here too. One, mentioning in the verse that we want to make some comment on, and that was going to be the subject of our concluding talk, or its going to help us to perform the topic for the concluding talk here this afternoon. Now, G-d says "We raised to degrees of wisdom whom we please, but over all endowed with Knowledge, is One, Only One, The All Knowing." This quote from Quran, in Qur'anic language arabic, fusha. "Above every possessor of knowledge, is the All Knowing, that's G-d, Aleem, knowing all. So, what is the message here? You ask anyone who reads the Quran, they know who it's talking about here. It's talking about G-d. Any Arabic speaking person, if you read this verse in Quran, you know it means G-d is one above all, who possess knowledge."

What is the situation there in that chapter? People who don't believe in G-d. People who think they're G-d. Pharaoh thought he was G-d. According to our Book, he said, "I know no lord but me, not answerable to anybody. I know no lord but me." That's what he said until he started drowning in the sea. And then He said, "I bear witness that the G-d of Moses is G-d."

And you know there's another comparison. Didn't that compare with us in the old mind. "Who is G-d?" the black man. The owner, the maker, the cream of the planet earth, father of civilization, god of the universe. You know we used to talk like that? And then when the whipping came on us, he said, "I know no G-d. No G-d but Mohammed's (pbuh)." We bear witness that there was no G-d but the G-d of Mohammed's, (pbuh) to whom the Quran was revealed. Yeah! We confessed. But we had to be put in difficulty, like Pharaoh. He was put in difficulty. He said, "hey I apologize Egypt, I know no G-d but the G-d of Moses. He's G-d. Above every possessor of knowledge is Aleem, The All Knowing."

Now, really, it's not right for any Muslim to call himself Aleem. Not ever Aleem. Aleem and something else, something that qualifies it. You can call yourself Abdul Aleem; you can call yourself Aleem Mujeed, or something like that. As long as you qualify it with something, it's ok. But just to say Aleem, no Muslim likes to do that. However, And An-Aleem is the attribute of G-d.

Although terms without even (An) on its decisions, language, shared compositions, or certain language on it will also clearly mean that G-d is that. That is not for any except G-d. Above every possessor of knowledge is the All Knowing. Aleem! Is One, Knowing All. Now, what is this to tell us?

Let me go to Moses now. Moses, in his search for knowledge. A certain kind of knowledge Moses was searching for. And he saw a fire at the foot of the mountain). And He told his people, he said, "I see a fire, so I will go there. Perhaps I will bring something to warm you by, or at least a light." He was interested in comfort and light. So he went there, and when he got there, G-d says, "Remove your shoe's, you're on sacred ground." He finally went up into the mountain to speak with G-d. And when He got up into the mountain to speak with G-d, He said, "O G-d, show me your face." And G-d said, "you cannot see me except that big mountain stands." And Moses, at that announcement fell into a swoon. He fainted. And when he recovered, the mountain crumbled down to sand, which means that He didn't see G-d He didn't see G-d's face. Many mentions of this, I used to hear it. "Moses talked to G-d face-to-face, as a man talking to a friend." And they're quoting the Bible. And when you read the Quran, Allah says in the Quran, "you cannot see me except that this mountain be removed." So, when he tried to behold G-d, he fainted. Now Moses swooned or fainted, he lost consciousness. Now, did Moses see G-d?

He didn't see G-d as He wanted to see G-d. But did he see G-d? Yes, he did see G-d, but he didn't see G-d with his rational vision, he didn't see G-d with his intellect. He saw G-d with his spirit. He saw G-d with his heart, and that's what made him faint. When he beheld G-d, his mind went blank. When he beheld G-d, his own thinking apparatus collapsed but did He see G-d? Yes, he saw G-d, but he didn't see G-d as he wanted to see G-d. Is that clear? And to prove that he didn't, it says." And when he recovered himself, the Mountain was crumbled to dust, right?". So G-d says, "You won't see Him, unless the mountain remains standing." So when he recovered, the mountain crumbled down like dust. So, what is the Mountain? A

Physical Structure. A mountain is a physical structure. So what G-d is saying, if you see me it will not be through the physical. The physical has to be removed. Yes.

So the proof that he didn't see him through the physical... because when he woke up, he saw the physical mountain had crumbled to dust. And G-d says, "in order to see Me, the mountain has to remain in place." So the hidden meaning here, the hidden message here is that he didn't see Him as he thought he could see Him, but never the less, he saw Him, because if he fell. The mountain in himself. The Mountain without, also fell. But the mountain of himself fell. He swooned and he passed out. His mountain fell, and crumbled as sand. And he did see G-d, but it was with his soul that he saw G-d, mot with the physical. So when he recovered his sight, the physical was not there so it had been changed. The mountain was removed. So, you cannot see G-d by that method.

But what is it telling us? Look at the mountain. The mountain comes up like this. Now what do you call this? The foot of the Mountain, and that's the head. How do you spell Head? HEAD, that's right. I started to spell it, HEED. HEED. Now, look, this is a mountain. The man goes up into the mountain in search of knowledge. Why use the mountain as a symbol? The mountain of yourself. The thinking apparatus is here in the top of the mountain. Vision is in the top of the mountain. The superior outlet is in the top of the mountain. The beholding the physical material is in the top of the mountain, so when you get up here in the top of the mountain... why does man use the mountain as a symbol? Because you can see pretty good down here, but when you climb up here and look, oh, your focus, and scope is so much broader. You see so much better, you see so much farther. When you go on top of the mountain. I've been on top of mountains, I know, I'm speaking from experience.

Ok, but look, small hills are not quite like mountains. If you go up a high mountain, you're feeling changes as you go up. The higher you go, the lighter the head gets. As you're going up you're heavy, but the higher you go, the lighter your head gets. Your head gets so light, that if you're not careful, you'll fall. Right? You get dizzy, you get a little woozy, like you're going to fall over, you know.

And another thing happens. Not only does your head begin to experience lightness but you begin to experience, colder, regions in the air. Right? It gets colder as you go up. It gets colder. Ok, so man gets up here, in the top of the mountain, and he's there on the peak.. He has found the point, the mountain point, the mountain peak. So he has narrowed down, to a small surface. He left the broad base down here. He left the broad base down there, and went up to a small, small foundation. A small foothold. Now, up here, he sees the remedy into the knowledge. His vision is broad, he sees more. He beholds the land like nobody can down here on the ground. And the atmosphere is lighter, and clearer up there. So he thinks himself very well situated, but what happens up here? Up here he gets in touch with his own possibilities for his intellect. He found the possibilities for his own intellect. So, when he gets up here and finds the possibilities for his own intellect, if he's not careful, he may think that all of this power to see this far, to watch over all that is happening here, to be above all others, all of this power may suggest to him that he's G-d. And that's what happens sometimes. Man arrives in his own intellect, in his possibilities of his own intellect, He thinks himself to be G-d.

But really, he's just came up into the higher levels of his own intellectual possibilities. Right? But he has also done something else. He has left the broad base. Was the fire in the top of the mountain, or was the fire seen in the base? So, when he observed the fire, the fire was at the foot of the mountain. It wasn't in the top. So the fire is a sacred fire. The sacred fire wasn't up there, the sacred fire was down here, on holy ground. That's in the base.

I hope you're reasoning with me. So let's go on with the fire. Say's, and the fire was burning, but the things that was in it, was not consumed, it wasn't eating up the things that were in it. They were holy people in it, but they weren't being burned by it. They were in that fire. So that's something too we missed. The holy fire was not in the top of the mountain. The holy fire was in the base of the mountain, but he went up to the mountain to speak to G-d, up on top of the mountain. He wasn't satisfied to speak to G-d in the base. He wanted to see G-d. Could he speak to G-d in the base of the mountain? Yes, because G-d spoke to him in the base of the mountain. He said, "take off your

shoes, you're on holy ground". But when he walked up
there, G-d said, " Hey, be careful, you're walking up, this
is Holy Ground.

Now, you're walking up the mountain of your own intellect
to see Me, and you want a face. So now G-d says, "above
everything." Understand that Moses represents the thirst
for knowledge , the freeing of the intellect, but for a
definite purpose. He wasn't Gnostic. The Gnostic s have
different purposes. The Old Gnostics who ruled
Christianity in the early days of the Church. Who hoarded
the knowledge and separated everybody else kept the
masses out of the knowledge. Enslaved the masses.
Talking about the early Church, they enslaved the women,
and they enslaved the masses. That Gnostic Elite era of
the early church.

Now, Moses is not that type. He wasn't looking for that
kind of Revelation. Moses was trying to find G-d with his
rational mind. The Gnostics, they believed that you had to
have divine spark in you, divine gifts from G-d. And
everybody couldn't get that divine gift. This is beliefs of

the Gnostics. They believed that to have that vision, that knowledge and that insight, that intelligence, that you had to be blessed with the ability. There had to be something divine in you, that's what they believed. And that the average citizen was not capable of that. And the average citizen could not be a part of their circle.

They should be reared with animals. That was their belief. Treat them kindly, they're G-d's animals. They're G-d's creatures. Treat them kindly, but don't give them any recognition on our plane. Knowledge is not for them. Knowledge is for us. For education, the freedom to have education came late in western civilization. Public education came very late in western civilization, in fact, just a century ago or less. Right? When the public was given the opportunity to have education, everybody could be educated. Even the women were not allowed to go to school and get educated. Women had to stay at home and do domestic chores around the house . They had no future in the leadership of the society. That was the Gnostics.

Moses was not like that. Moses was trying to bring his people up.

Moses was seeking G-d with his rational curiosity. Not with any spooky kind of intuitive ability to come into divinity like the Gnostics believed in. No, Moses was really trying to see G-d with his rational mind. Moses said to G-d, take the knot out of my tongue. Oh G-d, take the knot out of my tongue." What is the matter with his tongue? We used to think he was tongue tied. The knot in his tongue was the ignorance that kept him from being able to speak wisdom. The absence of knowledge that prevented him from speaking wisdom in a very clear, and articulate way with knowledge. So he wanted to be articulate. He wanted to be able to express the wisdom that he had some grasp of, but he didn't have the knowledge to put that wisdom into a language of the wise. So he asked, "O G-d, untie the knot in my tongue." So this is the kind of person Moses was.

He had been conditioned by Egypt, and Egypt conditioned him to want to see G-d in the body of a man, a physical body. Because Egypt had presented their base figures as divine figures, and their Pharaoh as the lord of the world. Yes, Pharaoh. His presence in Egypt was similar to the presence of Jesus (the body, the person in the body, in Christian society). He was lord and god, and he believed, they believed that there was an inheritance of divine office that came from G-d (the invisible), into the body of Pharaoh, (the visible). Now, isn't that similar to what the Christians believe now? That's what they believe. That's what Egypt believed, and G-d sent Moses against Egypt. So why don't you think that he's going to send somebody against America, and against Europe and every country that believes that Jesus in the body of a man is the son of G-d? Yes, he sent Mohammed (pbuh) against that. Allah say's through the mouth of Mohammed (pbuh), in this Holy Book here. Say to the Christians, "stop saying that G-d is three." Tell them it is best for them if they stop that, yes. So G-d did send somebody to stop it. And again G-d says in our Holy Book, "and let us come to terms that respect each other." The terms being that we do not make lords in our own bodies. Look how the Quran is revealing an injustice. That one people will say" this man in our race, is the son of G-d." What situation does that put the other races in? If a man of your race is the son of G-d, then it is the man of your race, and your race has been favored above other races. As it's intended to make other races look to you and your people as divine people and think of themselves as being the least of divine, because G-d didn't choose their color, or their race to present himself in. You have to shock these people out of this insanity because I believe in my heart, never will African Americans be equal to Whites, or Asians, or anybody, until they get that image of a white man being G-d out of their minds, alright! What wisdom did we get out of this? "Above every possessor of knowledge is the All Knowing, the one who possesses all knowledge."

This is to tell the Muslims, that the Muslim cannot come under any authority on the basis that, that authority is smarter than me. I don't care how much knowledge you possess. You possess knowledge, that doesn't give you right to dictate to me, or to be over me, or to enslave me and deny me my rights. Pass me around without me using my own thinking, my own ability to think. That doesn't give you any right, (because you have more knowledge, because you're big in the intellect). No! Because no matter how smart you are, you will never get smart enough to be G-d. Above every smart aleck is G-d. And that's what He said. I know what He said. Above every smart aleck is G-d. More of you need to know that. We need to know that and live by that.

We go on these campuses and let some arrogant intellectual change our whole mind; change our mind about what's morally right, change our minds about what's ethically right, change our minds about what's socially right. Turn our backs on our family, look at them like trash. Start doing devilish things. Join the crooks in the society, because some wise shrewd devil, pretending to be a great intellect, charms you, and overcomes your stupid jackass mind, and make you feel he's god. And you see the little stupid butt walking behind their professions and they're worshiping them, worshiping them. Pitiful, you and your jackass will never worship any successor. "Yeah, I'll be a jack-ass until G-d put an angel on my back and shows me a flaming sword or something. I ain't gonna worship no pretender." And that's what they are. They get a little knowledge and pretend to be much greater than they are. And they charm you, seduce you into believing that they're greater than they really are. And you say, "He knows it all. He's powerful." Some of us would rather say, that when you were a Christian, you would say, "I'd rather be a doorman in the house of G-d, than something here," you know. And there's some of us, we'd rather be shoeshine boy's for these professors than to be free in this community, helping to advance the cause of the poor, suffering people. You would rather shine their shoes, carry their bags for them.

Now, since we're on this symbol, the cross is another symbol. And actually, it's another way of saying mountain. But this is a different kind of mountain. One is a mountain that goes up from a broad base. Here is the mountain that goes up from a narrow base and it broadens out here in the chest area. It broadens out in the chest area, and then it gets small again in the head. Now, somebody will say, "well, you've never seen a mountain like that." Yes I have, you would be surprised. You haven't been to the right regions of the earth. I saw a mountain coming up like this, out of the ground, and it went out like this, and then like that. I've seen it. Say, "well, how is that possible?"

Water was here. And water just eroded the rocks, and the way water eroded the rocks, it left that mountain standing like that. Now, I don't know what water came against the church, but the black church certainly is out of shape. Now look! As the Serpent was lifted up in the wilderness, so shall the son of man be lifted up. Now, understand that Moses went up into the mountain, and it says, his people would just debate him almost into insanity. They wouldn't accept anything from Moses.

Why wouldn't they accept anything from Moses? Why, everything Moses said had to be questioned by his people? You who study the Bible, I heard a lot of preachers, preaching of the Bible, you know, Moses story. How come he had to take a lot of lip from his people. It is because he was a common man. Moses was a common man. He was not an intellectual. And when he followed his own rational urge to go higher into the knowledge by himself without tutors, without teachers with the degrees; when he came down from the mountain, with the knowledge, his ignorant people didn't want to recognize him because he didn't have the credentials of the elite. So they argued with him. Right? Now how come I get so much argument from my people. It is because I don't have a degree from Harvard, or Yale. Not even a degree from a little Junior College, (Kennedy King). I have no degree from any of these colleges. So what's wrong with you, you have to listen to him? Because for one thing, I don't get this kind of problem that Moses got. They spoke out to him in his face. None of you talk to me in my face, because you know G-d has blessed me to overwhelm you. So they don't talk to me in my face because they fear, that if they get in my face, they say, "hey, the man got ammunition. The man got qualifications, ammunition, and that ain't gonna come out good."

They don't talk challenge to me in my face, but I hear that they talk about me behind my back. "Oh man, you can't speak anything he says. He don't know what he is talking about. He don't have any degree from nowhere. I hear it, it comes back to me that my own people come here and they go back among each other and say these things about me. "He don't have no degree. He's not educated. He just talking." So why don't you tell me that in front of my face? And let's see who can talk. And you can't talk about what I'm talking about. Let's see who can talk and who can't talk.

And then I go around white people and they look at me, and they admire me, and they respect me. I go around the best of the white minds and they show, oh so much respect. And I humble myself around them, and it makes them uncomfortable. They say, "please, don't do that." Yes. Then I come around my own kind, and they think they know something. They say, "gone man." They say, "you worship the Imam." Well you see, it's not the same situation, but it's kind of like that situation. Well, because I don't have a degree, my people are always questioning, and attacking me behind my back. But they did it to Moses before his face.... wore him out. So Moses was given, blessed with something that would reach the ignorant masses minds.

He was blessed with a strategy, with a psychology - psychology and strategy. So Moses, he raised up a pole in the wilderness, and he put a symbol, or an emblem of a snake at the top of the pole. And he put it at the top of the pole. Dead! It was hung up there dead. And the Bible says, "and whenever his people beheld, (when they saw that sign), they were healed." Healed of what? Healed of their ignorance of attacking their leader all the time, unjustly, and without a knowledge base. They were healed of that foolishness. What was the message that he gave them in that sign?

If there is any Reverend's here, from your church; if you haven't been taught these things in your schools, please take notes. This is very valuable to you today. What is the message in that sign? The Message is this. "you stupid people, you want to be high and mighty (intellectually speaking or knowledge wise). You want to be at the top. take a lesson from the snake, the snake is wise. He trusts strategy. He trust's intelligence. The Bible says, "he's the most subtle creature. And another place it says the wisest of the creatures," the serpent. And again it says, "be like the serpent, wise but kind and humble like the dove." So in the Bible, the serpent is the symbol of wisdom. Is he hot headed like you? The Bible says, "and Moses' people

attacked him with fiery tongues. Fiery tongues, hot
head's."

Get all heated up in their hearts and minds and start
speaking nut language, and think they're wise. So Moses'
psychology was that, and here's the serpent. Now, look
how the serpent gets to the top of the pole. You want to go
to the top of the Mountain? You want to climb to the top
of the pole? You can't get up there hot headed. The snake
is cool bodied. Cool down, then you can get up there.
And once you get up there high enough, if you got the
mind, if you got the mentality, and the motivation, and the
composure of the serpent, once you get up there high
enough in the cold region, you become immobile.

Those who know snakes, when it gets cold enough, the
snake dies. He doesn't die really, he just becomes
immobile. He can't move, he can't do anything. But as he
warms up, he comes back to life. See, the higher you go in
the regions, in the heavens, the colder it gets. So you can
go up, but eventually it's gonna get so cold up there.
You're gonna become immobile. You're not going to be

able to do anything. You'll be as dead. How was Moses able to tell them that? Because he had experience. He went up the Mountain and he got up there to the top, and he was able to see the highest reality, and he became as a dead man. He was only giving them a sign of his own experience. He said "look I was once ignorant, and I went up the pole. I tried to go up to ascend the top, and I got up there to get the highest light and the region was so cold, and I was feeling so light, I fainted, I lost all control."

And he told them that. He reached the many among the masses, and they stopped, because they saw his logic, they saw his psychology. They stopped. They said, "yes, that's our weakness, that's our failure. We allow our conscious to blind our intelligence. We get hot headed. We start to argue, and the blood gets hot and blinds our own intelligence. They say, "O yeah, Moses is the right man. We should be cool if we want to get up, we gotta be cool if we want to get up and Moses let them know, "you cannot get up to G-d. You can only go up soh, then that intellect become as dead."

Now, the Bible says, "as the serpent was lifted up in the wilderness, so shall the son of man be lifted up." So what does it meaning now of Jesus being lifted up on a cross. We don't believe that. You know Muslims don't believe in that. We don't believe Jesus was crucified. He didn't die that way. But what does it mean to the Christians? We don't attack them. Now that I understand, I don't attack what they believe. If anything, I try to make them believe better.

So what does it mean? It means this, Moses, his role was to free the intellect. To bring his people into intellectual excellence. Growth and excellence. For he taught them a psychology that enabled him to reach the minds of the masses, and bring them into respect for the intellect, and into a posture, or position of mind's that will enable them to progress intellectually.

He brought them into a belief that these wild passions of ours go against the function of the intellect. That's what he taught, because the materials the serpent was made out of was brass. Yeah. You who know the Bible. The material the serpent was made out of (that he put upon the pole) was brass. Now, those who know something about metals.... G-d blessed me also to learn about metals, I'm a welder; I welded brass. When you put extreme heat to brass, it kills the quality of it. That's what he was telling them. The Bible's got science in it, like the Quran. The mental means more than that.

The dumb preachers just know the brass serpent, maybe he will. Look up brass and find it means bold, brazen. Maybe he knows that he'll be proud telling the congregation. And he thinks he's really got something, but he doesn't know anything about metal, maybe. But he's still without great knowledge, he's not a metal worker, Ok? So, the wisdom is that your mentality in the eye of the wise man, (your intellect, your rational possibilities) is like brass material. Gold, is the wisdom that G-d gives. Brass is the wisdom of man. And no matter how high, (what you try to do with it), if you go into extreme heat, it will burn out the quality of your brass. Isn't that true? Isn't that a great symbol? You who understand. Yes! If we give ourselves to passions, (I don't care if it's just the passions to be free, the passions to defend our life), if you give yourself to too much, to any passions other than the passion to love G-d, you're in trouble because the heat of that is gonna burn out the qualities of your good senses. After awhile, the heat gets too much, it burns out the quality of your good senses. Just like the extreme fire, extreme heat burns out the quality of the brass. And the Bible says, "and it becomes as tinkling brass." And I have hit brass with my welding rod after the quality has burnt out, and it sounds like dead metal. It becomes dead metal. Can't carry a good sound. But to Moses, He said, "but ascending up high, renders the intellect as dead." Now, extreme heat burns out the quality. It becomes dead by extreme heat, extreme cold. The serpent says he had two things here, working as one, didn't he? The serpent, and brass.

If you want to keep the quality of the brass, get out of the heat. But to get out of the heat, you've got to have the composure, and discipline of mind, that the serpent has. And if you get to far in the cold, the serpent is dead. Isn't that Islam? See, when you interpret these things rightly you come up with the purity of the message, and purity of the message is Islam. G-d says, "and there are those who do not give themselves to any extreme, but they take the moderate course" They follow the moderate line of reasoning. They don't give themselves to any extremes. They don't become wise, submissive people under the heat. And they don't become Gnostic, Saints, Puritan people, ignoring the needs of their society. They don't isolate themselves by thinking that they are a special class of pure beings, and they don't lose their lives in permissiveness, under the heat. But they take intelligent roles, which is the midway. Yes, this is Al-Islam. And if you understand what Moses is saying, he's telling them that principle. "don't try to go up so high, and come up empiricism. Don't try to go up too high because you will be dead."

And now, in what they call heat, I'm talking about the scientific discipline, that you do not let your human feelings come into your experiment, or into your work. Ok, so actually those who are able to do that work, don't they have to die to their own impulses? They have to die to their own intellectual impulses, and follow obediently, without letting your own influence, they say you can't become subjective. Subjective means you let your own self come into the picture. Right? Or let your own influence come in to the picture. You have to keep them out. And they call that true scientific discipline. Right?. Well, that's the same kind of discipline you need to come into the knowledge that G-d wants you to have, of the book. If the world tells you die to your own thinking, your own theories, your own motivation to become purely obedient to scientific discipline. And G-d tells you the same thing, to become purely obedient to divine discipline. Why should you say, "G-d wants us enslaved, the world wants you enslaved." Because G-d wants you to do that to improve you. To give you more from him. They want you to do that so you can serve capitalism. They make science for you to serve capitalism, and the rest, make them to serve communism.

they are the tools of capitalism, and communism. For those who serve G-d, are free. If you really know what G-d want for you, when you serve G-d, you're free. You're Free. G-d doesn't tell me, "believe in Me now Wallace." I know my name, you don't have to tell me. "You believe in Me now Wallace. You have to put down Shirley , you have to put down women, put down the world, devote yourself to nothing but holy things in this sacred house."

G-d didn't tell me that. I'm Free. G-d says, "His world is spacious. The possibilities for your potential are many. Go anywhere you want to go, just obey me. Just respect me, who made it all possible." So, none of us Muslims should be trying to make their children go to certain kinds of professions. We should just do what G-d did. Say, the whole world is open son. Find your interest, just be good. Just be right. Just be principled. Just be obedient to G-d".

The whole world is open son. Find your interest. That's freedom but some of us parents, we want to cut out a little role for our children. "Oh, I want him to be a dentist." That's what you want him to be. G-d is not possessive like that. Does that mean he's disqualified to be a dentist? Oh, that's what you want him to be. That's what I want him to be. "I want him to be a Dentist; oh, I want her to be a ballet dancer." And she might be wearing a size twelve shoe, and might be weighing 200 pounds. And you want her to be a ballet dancer. That's terrible.

If you really know this Religion, you wouldn't want anything else. Not ruling you. You wouldn't want anything else ruling you. If you really know this Religion, Allah rules us. The knowledge of G-d is my rule over all other rules. I'm happy with that. I'm free with that, and I find more respect in that. Yes, when you come into the world of knowledge, that's the way all of you will feel. The world has lied to us about Religion. Now, over all that possess knowledge, is "The Possessor, Who's All Knowing, is the Knowledgeable One who is All Knowing." For that tells us this, that no matter how high we go with the intellect, there's One above us, that's G-d.

Now, in conclusion, I want to say to you, just as G-d has pointed out the intellectual possibilities for man, when he can only go so high, and then he's dead, non-functioning. So, it is for every other essential goal, or aspiration in man. Some people look at the social factor and they say, "oh, the best way to raise man up is by supporting and encouraging social motivation." And they take on that kind of orientation. And they encourage that kind of orientation privately and sometimes publicly, to try to bring the people to their highest peak, and eventually they fail. They go down. None of them have lasted forever. They all failed. Some come into this so-called Gnostic awareness, like the early Church did after Jesus, (pbuh), and they encouraged that, encouraged that, getting the elite together, the hierarchy, the ivory tower of the brain people. They're really nothing but stupid people. And they encourage that, and support that.

But what has happened, they had to be overthrown by the Protestant movement, and by the Liberal Movement. Huh. They had to be overthrown, because they had become the oppressor. And the others would like at some other natural aspirations of some other natural urge is man, and they would think, " oh do we give our attention to this particular. Oh, we would make a greater society, we would have the greatest society." What G-d is telling us, "No, No, No!" Some people say, "oh, the G-d is in the working of all people working together." No! When you have a perfect society, with all people cooperating together to promote work, and productivity, that's G-d. No! G-d say's He is above all of His servants, all of His sorker's. So all these workers sticking together, they're not one, but who's above them?

They call the communist a society, organizations. The workers' society to bring us together in America. Let's organize the workers. Let's put him in unions. Let's organize the workers, the American workers movement. And the workers movement is to bring you into communism. Huh? That's what it is to do. It's to bring you into communism. Well, what kind of end, the workers movement comes to? It comes to an end. an end that produces nothing that it promises.

It promises the workers dignity. Has it produced it? No. We know for a fact it has not produced it. So what is G-d saying to us in the Quran? That there are certain top priorities, and that top priority for man, is G-d. And that's what is meant by Allah-U-Akbar. G-d is more important; G-d is greater; G-d is bigger; G-d is more important. For everything there is One above it. That is G-d. So no matter what we organize, if we don't recognize G-d. Again, what Allah says in the Holy Book, He says "Here's the great Hajj. The great Revelation of Hajj." When man brings his animals there, and he sacrifice them for the pleasure of G-d. Animals here are symbolic of his own social urges. And he sacrifices them to come into the social society that G-d wants on this earth. He sacrifices the animals. So what G-d says, "The blood reaches Me not." Oh, I'm gonna be saved by the blood of Jesus. "The blood reaches Me not." So for a Muslim, how are you gonna be saved by the blood of somebody, when the blood cannot reach G-d? "The blood reaches Me not. But your piety reaches Me. Your fear of Me, your love of Me, your discipline for My pleasure, it reaches Me. But your blood reaches Me not." Huh! that's what G-d says.

It's some great implications. Far reaching implications. On that subject alone, I can call Muslims that have the decency to admit the truth in the Quran away from communism, and away from Christianity because they're both are just twins of one kind of belief. That's all. In fact, they had a movement started a few years ago, by the blacks, and some whites too, to bring communal life in under the name of Christianity. Oh yeah, what Jesus really intended was socialism, communalism. Trying to use Jesus quietly to support communism. Yes. "The blood reaches Me not." They call the communist, the Red. "The blood reaches Me not. But your piety does." So if you favor, and you want this great social life in the society of human beings; we want social justice, social equality, and want social purity.

We want the greatest possibility for our social aspirations. And G-d has given us the way to the best, possible, society. In His Holy Book, Quran, He has given us the best possible way. So, we don't raise up any red flag as being the end for man, or green flag, or no other color flag as being the end for man. The end for man is colorless. It is obedience to G-d, and that has no color. Obedience to G-d. If it has colors, then it's all colors. Huh. And when you bring it all together, it becomes colorless. Like the light, how the light becomes all the colors. But they're combined in the light, and there is no color. Allah-U-Akbar. So we conclude this today on this note.

In our life, we must understand Allah-U-Akbar. No matter what we organize, or what we aspire too, nothing is possible for man that will transform man into G-d or eliminate the need for G-d in his life. No matter what we do, we cannot go so high that G-d becomes unimportant. No matter what we do, or how high we go, or how far we reach out, G-d will still be, top priority so thank you very much.

Again, As-Salaam-Alaikum. That is Peace Be Unto You. Let us read now, Al Fatihah. With G-d's Name, Most Gracious, Most Merciful. Praise be to G-d, The Cherisher and Sustainer of the Worlds. Most Gracious, Most Merciful. Master of the Day of Judgment. Thee do we Worship, and Thine Aide we Seek. Show us the Straight Way. The way on whom Thou hast Bestowed thy Grace. Those whose portion is not Wrath, and who Go not Astray. Ameen. A-Man.

Now, we have a serious correction to make before going into the tenth section of the Surah, the chapter of the Quran, titled Joseph, or Yusuf, in Arabic. Joseph, peace be unto the Prophet. And that correction is the report, concerning (in the Quran) the mountain, where Moses asks G-d to show Himself. "G-d, let me see You" he said. And you know at first, I said, that the mountain did not remain standing, then I had second thoughts and I said I wasn't sure. So we got some help from the audience too, and they were feeling the same as I felt, (that the Mountain did remain standing). That was our position, that it remained standing. We were wrong. The first report was correct, or quotation was correct. That is the Mountain did not remain standing.

What I was thinking, (since I couldn't) My thoughts were rushing, and that happens. I was thinking that the sign, was only in Moses not remaining himself, on his feet. He swooned, when he saw it. He swooned. But also, the mountain did not remain standing. Now, we're gonna read this again for the purpose of correcting our mistake. And remember, all of us, to keep Allah in mind, and asking Him for protection from the rejected Satan. Because G-d says "even to the Prophet." Now, you know, we're no Prophet. You don't have that protection that the Prophet had. And that high achievement that the Prophets had. And G-d said to even the Prophet (pbuh), He said, "Seek G-d for protection from the rejected Satan" and He said, "That if he should cause you to cause something to be put in,

That G-d hasn't authorized, G-d will remove it." Now, even the Prophet, he's vulnerable to make a mistake, because of the influence of a Satan. But G-d protected the Quran. He said, "if he should cause you to put something in, unauthorized, He said, it will be removed." G-d will remove it. So we don't have anything in the Quran except what G-d authorized. It is because G-d Himself, protected it, and protected the Prophet (pbuh). It doesn't mean that something didn't come into the Prophet (pbuh).

That's why G-d is saying this, because G-d was telling The Prophet, "now something is in you now that is not in agreement with this, and this is the influence of the Satan but don't worry, G-d will take it out." So G-d took it out, and we didn't get it. When Prophet Muhammad (pbuh), gave it to us, it was without any flaws, or mistakes. So let us read the correction now. And all of us, let's remember to always keep our own limitations on our minds that we can make mistakes, and when you're reading the Quran, and ask, G-d to protect us.

The correction is in the chapter, The Heights, the seventh chapter. And the verse is the one hundred forty third verse. I'll read it now. When Musa came to the place appointed by us, and his Lord addressed him, He (Musa) said, "Oh my Lord, show Thyself to me, that I may look upon You". He, (G-d) said, "you will never see Me, but look unto the mountain. And if it remains firm, in its place, then you shall see Me." When his Lord manifest, that means made clear, showed him. Manifested His glory on the mountain, (showed Moses the glory of G-d on the mountain), He made it (the mountain) as dust. He made the mountain as dust. The mountain did not remain stable, (as we made the mistake in saying). He made it as dust, and Moses fell down in a swoon. He (Moses) said, when he recovered his senses, "glory be to You O G-d. To You I turn in repentance, and I am the first to believe."

Now listen. we gave this mainly to make the correction, but look what Moses said to G-d after that experience. "I turn to You in repentance." What had he done wrong? He had regarded G-d as creation. He wanted to see G-d as we see creation. He had regarded G-d as creation, and he repented of that when G-d showed him the great wonder.

So the mountain did not remain in its place, the mountain turned to dust "as to dust."

G-d says "if the mountain remains stable, in its place, then you shall see Me." So it didn't remain stable in its place, it became shaky. Shaky and crumbled down like dust or something, or sand, it crumbled down. So it did not remain in its place. The mountain did not remain in its place. So here is Moses. Moses, it's his own intellect, the intellect of Moses was trying to see G-d as we see physical reality, or material realities. And the intellect of Moses, upon seeing the higher truth, the higher reality, became as though he was swooning, blanked out. He was cut off from that kind of approach to the material reality. He was trying to see the divine reality. He was cut off, his mind couldn't take it. So it was cut off from the approach to the material reality and his mind became spiritual. And as his mind became dominated by the spiritual reality, he could no longer hold his position there, trying to examine the material reality, and he fell into a swoon. fell into a faint.

So his intellect could not withstand an approach to a reality of G-d, as you approach material reality. Alright, swoon! He fell down and couldn't stand up. And the mountain also, he saw the mountain. First he saw the mountain losing its stability, losing its stability and crumbling down. What is the mountain? The logic, the material logic. The material logic fell down crumbled, before his face. "I'm trying to find G-d, and trying to see G-d based upon my material logic." The mountain, . the material logic. Going up into the heights of material logic. And the Mountain, (right before his very eyes), while he was trying to use that as a test to G-d, it failed. It lost its stability and crumbled down and when he saw the material logic upon which he himself was supported, his intellect was supported by the material logic, then he himself swooned, and fell down.

Now, it's very clear, because G-d has made it very clear. We just missed it. We missed it, but it's very clear in the Quran, because Allah has made it very clear in the Last Revelation to Mohammed the Prophet (pbuh). Allah, G-d has revealed the truth. But don't forget that in the conclusion of that, Moses said, "I turned to You in Repentance." And that's to tell the reader (those who seek an understanding) that there is sin on the part of man to try to reduce everything, (even G-d) to his own examination and experiments. That's a sin.

But Moses wasn't really guilty of that. He was guilty of being under the influence of Egypt, and under the influence of his rebellious people. He was a product of them. So his whole search was a search to get out from under the influence of Egypt, and out from under the ignorance of his people. So seeing that in that great wisdom on Mount Sinai, on the great mountain, caused him to see the mistakes of the intellect. The errors of the human intellect that is dominated by material. And he repented of it and then he went back down to give his people the commandments and the right guidance. And what started? Trouble! They started arguing with him. "Hey, where this guy been? Where he's been all that time up there?"

So, when he got down there, when he got back down they had gotten into their thing. building another idol. Building the Idol of Egypt, the golden calf. He had to go down and deal with that problem. And they just kept giving him arguments. Arguments because his mind was in the higher realm, and they were still in the lower realm, of material vision, or material possession. So that concludes that.

Now let us go back to our topic that we have been on, which is Joseph. Yusef, or Joseph in English. Chapter 12, and I believe we were on Section 10. Seek refuge from the rejected Satan. With G-d's Name, The Gracious, The Compassionate. Verse 80. Now, when they saw no hope of his yielding, they held a conference in private. The leader among them said, "know you not, that your father did take an oath from you in G-d's name, and how before this, you did fail in your duty with Joseph. Therefore will I not leave this land until my father permits me, or G-d commands me, and He is the best to command, (that is G-d is the Best to Command)." The next verse, "return you back to your father and say, oh our father, behold, your son committed theft. We bear witness only to what we know, and we could not well guard against the unseen."

So now, you know we left off where Joseph planted the King's cup. The King's beaker, the silver cup. He planted the cup in the saddle bags of his brother, his whole brother. He had only one whole brother by his mother and the father, Jacob. And the other brothers were the half brothers of Joseph. So he wanted his full brother with him. So he devised a plan, a scheme, to get his full brother with him. And the scheme was to plant the kings beaker, or the kings cup on Benjamin, on his brother.

The Quran doesn't give his name as Benjamin. The Bible gives his name as Benjamin. To plant the cup on his brother, so he would have an excuse to have his brother held for a crime. Held back in Egypt for a crime. And the Quran gives us the word of G-d, say's to us, "there was no way for him to stay in Egypt, (for Benjamin, his brother to stay in Egypt)." He had no other route to take because the law wouldn't permit his brother to stay in Egypt. But if he got him arrested, then he would be in Egypt. So he planned a way to get him detained in Egypt by planting the Kings beaker on him.

And now we're reading where they're having difficulty now, deciding how they're going to deal with the father, who had trusted them first with Joseph, and they failed the father's trust. And now they talked him into trusting them with the younger brother and he trusted them again, so they are now worried. No! He didn't trust them. Pardon me, but he was in their care, and they are now worried. He had suspicions, he had doubt's all the time about them being worthy of taking care of the younger brother, since they had failed with Joseph. And now, they are being advised by a leader among them to go back to their father and talk to him, talk over the situation with him.

The next verse says, "ask at the town, where we have been, and the caravan in which we returned, and you will find we are indeed telling the truth." So they're trying to convince the father now, that they are telling the truth. Now Jacob said, "no, but you have yourselves contrived a story good enough for you, so patience is most fitting for me. Maybe G-d will bring them back, all to me, in the end for He is indeed, full of knowledge and wisdom." And He turned away from them and said, "how great is my grief for Joseph." And his eye's became white with sorrow and he fell into silence, melancholy. Into a silent loneliness, sadness and loneliness. They said, "by G-d, never will you cease to remember Joseph, until you reach the last extremity of illness, or until you die." So they were not of the opinion of the father, that's regarding the value of Joseph. They said, "O, this man worrying himself to death, gonna kill himself, worrying about Joseph." Because G-d said, "they didn't put much value on Joseph." They thought Joseph to be of no value, very cheap. They esteemed him very lightly. they valued him very cheaply. He said, "I only complained of my distraction and anguish to G-d, and I know from G-d that which you know not." So here, obviously Jacob had more knowledge of revelation, more knowledge of the ways of G-d than his sons. He said, "I know of knowledge what you know not. O my sons, go you, go ye, and inquire about Joseph and his brother and never give up hope of G-d's soothing mercy. Truly, no one despairs of G-d's soothing mercy, except those who have no faith."

Then, when they came back into Joseph's presence, they said, "O exalted one, distress has seized us, and our family We have now brought but scanty capital, so pay us full measure we pray thee, and treat it as charity to us, for G-d does reward the charitable." So they're saying that they are in financial difficulty. They don't have much, and they have been distressed because of family problems and they're pleading to Joseph now, their younger brother, who G-d had blessed to get in a good situation in Egypt. G-d had blessed him to be put over the store houses by the chiefs of Egypt. So He said, "Know you how you have dealt with Joseph and his brother, not knowing what you were doing." Now here the Quran is saying that they did what they did in ignorance. The word in Arabic is antum jayhiluna, means, "because you were ignorant." What they did against Joseph and against the younger brother of Joseph, their half-brother. Two half-brothers, Joseph and his younger brother said that they did it in ignorance. So here we find that the brothers are being charged with doing a great sin, but at the same time we're being told that they did it in ignorance. They did it in ignorance. Ignorance caused them to do that. To do those things.

Their reasoning was faulty, and led them to commit sin. But they were trying to justify their actions, their wrong doing on the strength of their logic. On the strength of their logic, because you recall them saying, "O, let's do this to Joseph now. We will have enough time later to repent to G-d." So they were planning on repenting later, but they were doing a wrong at the present time. Presently they were committing a great wrong, with a hope that in the future they could make thing right again. So the cause is ignorance. Now, what is that? What is that talking about? It is talking about what they call expedience. Expedience. When you have an aim in mind, and you want to reach it, sometimes you run into moral conflict. And moral conflict will say, "you shouldn't take that advantageous step." Though it's very advantageous, it will bring you great results in reaching your purpose, or your object, you shouldn't take it, because there's a moral violation here. But moral expediency will dictate, material expediency, or political expediency will dictate, that you sacrifice the morals, presently for the great object down the road.

Nations do that. Local governments do that. That's a big problem for society, and government, a big problem. Allah is saying, in the Quran, "It's wrong. It's wrong." No matter how great the prize is down the road, you don't violate those rights. You don't make moral violations to get the advantage. No that's wrong, but some people in Religion, they believe that this is acceptable. They say, "O, you know they have many, but don't have to go to Religion. Go right to our own worldly expression" All is fair in love and war." That's a very popular saying. spoken by some of the wise, ignorant people of the west. right. "All is fair in love and war" Well, that's not right. That lead people to become devils and they have a saying in Religion, you know. "If the ends justify the means, then it's ok." So they're saying, if the end is great enough, it can justify the little wrong they do to get there. That's wrong. The Quran does not accept that.

So Joseph was one that the Quran holds up. Allah is holding Joseph up in scripture as being one that didn't have that spirit in him to sacrifice right, and principle to get an advantage. He'd rather suffer. And he had a lot of suffering, but look what was his end. In the end, he was put over those that used those tactics. Those who subscribed to that kind of methodology. Joseph was put over them. So let's go on with the reading now. And believe me, I'm giving you this in hopes that we will become a stronger people. I'm talking about the African

American People. A people stronger in moral make-up, moral commitment, and moral make-up, because that's what has us down now in the bad situations we're in. If our people had remained morally firm, morally together, we could have progressed so much my now. We'd be so far. We wouldn't be under these newcomers, Cubans and others. No, we would be advanced in every way beyond them. If we had just kept our moral life in some kind of good condition. But we left it, and right now, you know why that don't like me? Giving me the silent treatment. They're not going to talk to you openly. But they're giving me the silent treatment. And I'm sure they're whispering among themselves. "Wallace is not with us. Imam Warithudeen is not with us." And he has created a situation where the enemy is using him now, against us." I'm sure they talk that kind of talk. But what have I done? What have I done to betray them? I stood up for right. I won't join the black position if it's morally wrong. I'm trying to follow the Quran, I'm trying to follow my right guidance and if that causes me to have differences with black leadership, then we just have differences. You need somebody to differ because they are not speaking for all of us, no indeed.

It continues now. They said, "are you indeed Joseph?"
They're just beginning to really believe that this one that
they've been coming to for help is their brother now. They
said, "are you indeed Joseph?" He said "I am Joseph, and
this is my brother." So he told them, "yes I am Joseph, and
this one that I kept back here is my brother." He said his
full Brother. "G-d has indeed been gracious to us all.
Behold, he that is righteous and patient." Never will G-d
suffer the reward to be lost of those who do right." Says,
"whoever is righteous and patient." And Allah says over
and over in the Quran, "surely G-d is with the patient."
People who hold their patience, who do not give up their
patience, you give up your patience, you'll do anything.
Then you start making decisions without caring. They
said, by G-d indeed, G-d has preferred you above us and
we certainly have been guilty of sin." Now see, a people
that will admit their sin when they see the light of truth,
then there is forgiveness for them. So Allah treats them as
people who quickly grab the logic, and had their eyes on
really a great gain for themselves. Sacrificed the morals in
hope that they would make up for it later.

He excused them as being ignorant. Ignorant of moral logic. Their moral logic was faulty. So they were ignorant of the sound moral logic. So G-d treats them as such. I'm gonna go a little step further and say this. many Religions make this mistake. Many churches make this mistake. Now we have even Mosques, and Imams making this mistake. So let us understand then, if we are wise enough to see that some of the Religiousleaderships are violating moral principles to get their community, their church stronger, for an advantage to their church or to the religious propagation, let us have the same patience with them that G-d is having with these, that sinned against Joseph. What good is this if it doesn't serve us? Now, here it's saying we're tested. We're gonna be tested now. We who believe that we shouldn't sacrifice that moral, we shouldn't violate that moral. Let us have patience with those who do. Don't you know Farrakhan is not the only bad man out there. Most of them are the same. But the only thing, they're bad in degrees. As a Muslim, we're obligated to check another man who says he's a Muslim, and then he preaches something, or projects something, that gives us a wrong image. We're obligated to correct him. We're obligated to correct him. But even have patience with him.

But there are many religious denominations, or religious organizations. denominations of Jews, and Christians, and others, who violate the moral logic in order to advance themselves in a situation where they're encountering opposition from people that doesn't belong to their faith, or their religion. So as long as they're not really going too far extremes and we see that their interest is to advance right, but they're only using instruments of faulty logic, or breaking the moral principal or sacrificing principal sometimes. We are not to demand that everybody be perfect, or that everybody be morally correct all the time. (they have no moral sin on them). If we would reject all the people that have moral sin on them, or that sacrifice principal for advantage, it wouldn't be anybody to accept. So that's the great lesson here. The great lesson here, is that as long as the people have good intent, their purpose is good. As long as their purpose is good. If they're doing things that violate the moral logic, then you understand, in light of what G-d has revealed, that is wrong. And G-d wants people that won't do that. He wants people that are like Joseph. He wants people that won't do that. But at the same time, let us have patience with those who have those faults.

That's why I want cooperation. I want us to cooperate with Christians, Jews, and everybody else that wants to keep respect for G-d in Society, and respect for decent principles in society. I know they're not perfect. I know they do a lot of wrong. So do we? I'm trying to do my best, and I pray Allah, I don't get weak and start taking up the strategy of double logic. I hope I keep it pure. I don't intend to do that and I don't think I ever will, but I will have patience with those that do, as long as they are not notorious sinners.

Now Joseph tells his brothers, (because he knows of that situation with Jacob, the old man, the father), he tells them how to go back now, and get things straightened out. He says, "go with this, my shirt, and cast it over the face of my father. He will come to see clearly. Then come you here to me together with all your family." All Right! Now, this shirt is a mystic symbol (the shirt itself). It's a mystic symbol for the true report of what G-d revealed. That's Joseph's shirt. Joseph's shirt was the true report of what G-d wanted.

What G-d intended for man. What G-d had revealed. So, Joseph's insight was needed for his father. His father had great intellect. The old man represented the great intellect, the great powerful intellect that is universal. He saw all around, everything. His father was circumspectual. He had great vision, all around vision. And he could guide the youngsters very well, but he had lost the ability to interpret the G-d plan, or to gain insight into G-d schemes, and G-d plan. He had lost that. That's why the description is given of his eyes. That his eyes had become pale. Very pale, very white with sadness. But that sadness, there is also loneliness. The separation from what he wanted. He wanted Joseph. That's what he wanted, Joseph.

Joseph is symbolic of that ability to see into things. That interpretive vision, ability, great insight into the hidden mysteries of things. He had been separated from that. And actually the child he wanted was that. He wanted that ability. And he got the wife, Rachel, she's called in the Bible. And the purpose was to get from her... get from Rachel, who's symbolic of scripture.... Rachel, herself was symbolic of scripture - to get from her, Joseph who would be able to interpret ate the scripture. the son of scripture would interpret the scripture. So he wanted the Joseph by Rachel, who would have the great insight into scripture. So He would have a son that could interpret the scripture for Him.

He was a man of great intellect, but he hadn't been blessed with the vision to see into the mysteries of G-d's scheme, G-d's great scheme and plan. He was lacking that moral consistency and continuity in his vision. But he didn't have any bad intent. He was a man of good intent. But look at the boys he produced. The boys that would either threaten the prize that he wanted, (the great prize he was seeking), and that was Joseph. So you know the vision, (we're gonna try to cover this and complete this today). We'll complete the whole chapter today.

The vision that Joseph had, G-d told Joseph, according to the Quran, (he didn't tell him directly, but it says in the Quran, of Joseph), he would be given the ability of interpretation. G-d was gonna give him the ability of interpretation. And later, Allah says in Quran, that He gave him, (when he reached a certain stage in his growth and development), the ability of interpretation. That he had the ability to interpret some of the great reports of the sayings concerning G-d. Revelation.

And then he had the power of analytical insight. (into the nature of people), their souls, and their mental problems, or their psychological difficulties that they were having. And he was a doctor on his brothers, or his companions, in the jail, you will recall. So he had this power that G-d blessed him with, and not only the power to look at a piece of writing, and see into it, see the hidden things in it, but he could also hear your problems.

You could tell him your problems and he could see the hidden things in you. In your make-up. In your spiritual make-up. in your psychology, and your psychological make-up. And he could suggest to you ways to get yourself out of your bad situation. So all of this was a blessing to Joseph, and caused Joseph to be put up higher and higher until he was put over the storehouse, over the distribution of goods.

The shirt is taken back, and cast over the face of the old man. (I'm saving time by just giving it myself, without reading), And right away, Allah says in Quran, "his vision came clear" because Joseph's shirt was put over his face. So, it's all symbolic and poetic, very beautiful. The shirt being put over his face. So, you imagine a shirt being put over his face, his vision was blotted out, right. In other words, his vision was blotted out. Everything outside was just blotted out, and the shirt was over his face. So it's saying, the shirt was a healing. The shirt, first the truth from G-d, blocks out everything else. You have to see a new, all over again, because if you have your attention on anything outside of what G-d is showing you, it will only confuse the vision. So the shirt blocks it all out, and he comes into vision anew. And he sees very clearly.

And it goes on to say, as he begin to anticipate the nearness of Joseph. Just the shirt coming to him, he could sense it. Now, some of us don't believe in extrasensory perception, but I do. And many of us do. Some of you don't. You don't believe nothing. But even before the shirt got there, the old man, (because of his great intellect, his powerful intellect), he sensed the nearness of it. And he began to come back to life and the language he used, his son said, "Oh, you're getting back into your old clever mind again." They sensed that he was getting lively again you know, and he had a very clever mind, Jacob did. So finally the shirt was put over his face, and his vision came back very clear.

And let's see if we can sum these verses up now. Such is one of the stories of what happened unseen. So here, the word unseen is used for things that were not commonly known, or were known only to a very few. It was not public knowledge, so it is called unseen too. Unseen is used for "that which was revealed by inspiration unto you." Unto you means unto Muhammad now (pbuh). "Nor were thou present with them when they concerted their

plans together, in the process of weaving their Plot."
Mohammed (pbuh) was not there.

He was not present. That was many, many generations
before Mohammed's (pbuh) time. But G-d had revealed all
of that to him. Say, "even thou G-d has revealed all this to
you Mohammed." And they know, their learned ones
among them, in their hierarchy of the religion. They know
that what you have been given here is the truth. But it
says, "Yet no faith will the greater part of mankind have,
however ardently, thou does desire it." G-d is telling
Prophet Mohammed (pbuh), "no matter how passionately,
how strong you desire it, that they see the truth, they're not
people to have faith." So don't worry about them. The
majority will not have faith. The majority are not
grounded upon faith. They're grounded upon greed."And
no reward does thou ask of them, for this. It is no less than
a message for all the world's." So this great insight into
the mystery of Joseph and his brothers, the story of Joseph
and his brothers.

G-d is saying, Prophet Mohammed, I have revealed this to you, and you're giving it, (you're not asking anybody for a penny). You don't want any advantage, you want no reward for it. And you think that they should turn and be happy, and should become believers and should show faith, and correct their ways? That's the goodness of your heart. Most people are not that way. That's what G-d is telling Mohammed (pbuh). And how many sign's in the heavens and the earth do they pass by. Yet, they turn their faces away from them. And most of them believe not in G-d, without associating others with Him, and that's the truth. They don't believe in G-d, unless they associate some fantasy, or some trick. Some instrument for achieving what they want and that's a direct route to the pockets of the poor and ignorant people. Do they then feel secure from the coming against them of the covering veil, of the wrath of G-d, or of the coming against them of the final hour, all of a sudden, while they perceive it not?

Say thou, Oh Mohammed, "this is my way. I do invite unto G-d on evidence as clear as seen with one's eyes." See there. So you should understand this now. What has been given in this Quran concerning the mysteries of revelation,

(Joseph and his brothers), etc. Though it seems to us on the surface, a poetic story. If you are blessed by G-d, you can follow your rational urge, and you will see explanations, and conclusions that will explain that mystery clean out of all mysteries, into true reality. Every day, good sense, that's what it's saying. But how many will get it?

Prophet Mohammed (pbuh) wasn't sent to give us mysteries. He was sent to address mysteries to bring us into good, plain, sense knowledge. And look what it says now, "Say thou, this is My way, straight. I do invite unto G-d on evidence clear, as the seeing with one's eyes. I and whoever follows me." You hear that? So, if I'm an Imam, I'm charged to do the same. Right? I shouldn't lead the people with just symbols and mysteries. He says, "he invites to G-d on evidence that is clear as seeing with the eyes." Isn't that the promise of G-d to the people in scripture. Say, "and every eye shall see G-d's promises in scriptures that came before, that He shall bring the truth so clearly, (that every eye shall see)." Now, it didn't say every two eye's shall see. See, you have a left eye, and a right eye, "every right eye shall see." Now look what G-d says, clearing up the matter. "nor did we send before you as Apostles, (that is Prophets, or Messengers), any but men, mortals, (flesh and blood men)."

We didn't send anybody to be a spook, to be an Angel, to be other than human nature. To bring the people some kind of idea, of a vision, that is only possible for them, if they stop marrying and stop having children, and stop having sex, and stop wanting to make money. Get out of business, and just devote themselves solely to spiritual disciplines. Then you will come into the great truth that G-d has for you. No! Allah is clearing that up. No, not only for You Mohammed, is it given, so it can be seen clearly, but to all the men we sent before you. We sent them for the same purpose. Maybe they were not able to do it, but that was our intent. Some of them, they had to grow up. Prophecy and the office of Prophet is a progression. It started with Adam, we believe as Muslims, and it progresses. As it progresses, the vision, the correct vision of reality, of matter, and the whole reality, and the correct way of conceiving G-d, and divinity is to come home. To come home to the mind of the person when they're not burdened by any mysteries anymore.

Shouldn't be burdened by mysteries. It should come home clearly, that was the objective. But to achieve that objective, G-d had to grow humanity up step-by-step, from the lowest level of the potential in man, starting with Adam. Urge in man and grow him up, and grow him up to the fullness -- to Mohammed (pbuh)! Let's complete this. "Whom we did inspire." Men living in human habitation, not men living in caves. A lot of these Guru's and modern Sages, they want to live in a dungeon somewhere, in a rock somewhere, way away from civilization. No, No, that's not what G-d intended. He sent men Messenger's, rational men, who lived in human habitations. They didn't live in caves or deserted places for Monks, and Hermits. "Do they not travel through the earth and see what the end of those before them was? But the home of the hereafter is best for those who do right. Will you not then Understand?" Now, you would think that those people who separate themselves from social life, marrying, and business and all of that; you would think that they really, regarding the hereafter.

As a great goal, the greatest, right. You would think that. But look how the church, in the early history of Christianity, look how, under Gnosticism the church became, Acetic. Like the old fashioned Catholic way. Catholic Church. Catholic Hierarchy. Even now, the Catholics, they live a life of celibacy, most of them. Yes. They live a life away from the world, and no marriage, and no children. Well, there was a time before Protestantism, before Martin Luther. Protestant revolution. That was the order for Christianity. And during that time, the masses were like slaves. The masses were like slaves. No public education. Women couldn't go to school. Poor people couldn't get any education. In fact, the great majority of people did not get any education. It was hoarded by the Gnostic hierarchy. Yes, this is History.

Now, were they poor? They were wealthy. Catholics are wealthy now, but they were even more wealthy then. The wealth of the nations where they ruled was in their hands. It was in their treasures. Now, if they were so absorbed in the desire for the hereafter, what were they doing with all that, here and now? So our Holy Book exposes them. Don't you think these people that separate from women, and separate from all that, don't you think they are all sincere. If their mind has gone wrong in the social life, most likely has gone wrong also, in the rational life. Yes. so G-d says, "respite will be granted, until when the Apostles give us hope." G-d will allow this kind of thing to continue.

He won't wipe them off the face of the earth. He will leave them around here, in hopes that their ways will be changed. But the time will go on, and on, and on, to even the Prophets of G-d will fear to almost give up hope. And I'm sure the best one among us, the saints in Chicago Masjid, this Masjid. Some of you feel like almost at the point of giving up sometimes, don't you? I know you do. I do too. Say, "where is an end to this thing." But have faith in G-d. We'll be the winners in the end, dead or alive. That's right. Doesn't mean we're gonna see it, but dead or alive, we'll be the winner. Say, "give up hope, give up hope that their people will ever change, and that they will come to think they were treated as liars." Isn't that a burden on a Prophet to know that he has the truth? To know, with all of his soul and mind, that G-d has given him this but he's worried that he's going to die, and these people will write him down as a liar. That's a terrible burden. There reaches them our help eventually, and those whom we will, we deliver unto safety, and never will be warded off our punishment from those who were given to sin."

So, G-d is giving assurance to us. Don't worry. Even the Prophets have moments of despair, where they want to give up. They tend to give up hope. But don't worry, G-d did not let His Prophets down. Eventually, He showed them the victory. And the wrong doers will meet their just punishment. So don't worry, keep faith. There is in their stories instruction for men, endured with understanding. instructions for men that have been given the blessing of understanding. It is not a tale invented, but a confirmation of what went before it. A detailed exposition of all things, and a guide and a mercy to any such person, as would have faith.

And that is the conclusion of the chapter on Joseph. We think Allah, and we pray that we will have patience enough with the great wisdom that He's given to us in the

Quran, that we will rely on that wisdom in our times of trouble, and anguish. Seems like we're ready to give up hope. Pray G-d will bring these things to be remembered in our minds, and that we will remain faithful, and patient, and trust the wisdom, the great revelation, the great wisdom and insight, that G-d has given us as Muslims, in this Quran. And in the life of Mohammed The Prophet (pbuh), because with this, we can meet any challenge from anywhere, at anytime. All we need to do is grow up to this. We're not impoverished. We're not deficient. Only in our lacking, in growing up to this. That's all.

Believer's, that's all we need. With this, we can start off small. The same kind of concerns we have here, our Mosque, our school, the effort of business, promoting the effort of business, start off small. Politics and government, start off small, and move up, day by day, week by week, month by month, year by year, into the system. Move up! Keep going up, and up, and up. And don't tell everybody everything. But just get it. I share with you all, because if I don't share with you all, who am I gonna share with? I don't have anybody else that have faith, to sit and listen to me. So I share with you all. I share with my audience.

But now, you'll be blessed. many of you are educated, and you'll be blessed as you study the Quran, and become more familiar with it as you learn the Arabic, so you can read it in the original language, and you get a good Arabic dictionary, that'll show you how to check the meaning of everything.

You'll be able to become, yourself, a person blessed with great insight. Many of you, when you get it, don't tell everybody, but you think about it. Think about, and say, "now, how can I put this wisdom into practice without revealing the instrument?" You don't want to reveal the instrument to everybody. They don't deserve it. So how can I put this knowledge into practice without revealing the instrument? And then you put it into practice and grow your people up, so that we won't have to think of ourselves as a deficient and weak people depending on others all the time. This is the key, believe me. It isn't coming from anywhere else. I believe that Allah has intended this for us. It came to The Honorable Elijah Muhammad. It came to him, and he was attracted to it, and he became very courageous because of it. Now , it has come to his son, and his son has brought it into the universal meaning and context, (and it's intended for the black man of America).

I believe that with all my heart and soul that this Book came to the Honorable Elijah Muhammad, and now his son, and now to you, because G-d wants to deliver us from our stagnation, with the rope of this Book. This is what He's going to hand out. Let this rope down into the pit of black deficiencies, and stagnation. And we're gonna grab this rope, and we're gonna come up on the surface of the land. We're gonna get on the land. We're gonna stand up on the firm land, with this Book. And we're not gonna have to write Arabia, for help with it. All the help is gonna come right from here, that's right. Oh yes, and I'm convinced of that with all my life and soul. With all the fiber of my being, I'm convinced that that's G-d's intent. That's His purpose that He's going to fulfill. Oh Yes! Allah-U-Akbar.

So, Insha Allah, we'll meet again next Sunday. No, No, I won't be here, I'll be in Los Angeles, we'll meet the following Sunday, two weeks from today, at the same time, about a quarter to One. In fact we should be in time for Prayer around Eleven Forty Five. We should have Prayer here, and we will be over in the library over there, for Arabic and Religious Studies at 10. And we will stay there until Prayer time, and then we will come over here. If you don't care to join the Class, it's ok. If you come, just come here and make your prayer's, and wait here for us. We'll be here about time for Zhur Prayer. If you want to come join the class, you're welcome. I don't care how many. If it gets too big, we'll find some way to put black boards around the walls here. Because after all, there's no house of prayer in our religion, that doesn't accommodate also, the house of knowledge. It must be prayer and education all the time. That's what the Prophet did, (pbuh), and that's what we have to do. Ok, so thank you very much. Let's conclude with Dua. Al-Fatihah. Just Arabic this time. We gave the English in the Beginning.

ABOUT THE AUTHOR

Imam W. Deen Mohammed was unanimously elected as leader of his community after the passing of his father in 1975; the Honorable Elijah Muhammad, founder, leader, and builder of the Nation of Islam.

At a very early age, Imam Mohammed developed a keen scholastic interest in science, psychology and religion. He began his education, from elementary through secondary school, at the University of Islam in Chicago. Further educational pursuits took him to Wilson Junior College, where he concentrated on microbiology and to the Loop Junior College where he studied English, history, and the social sciences. However, his primary education has come from, and through, his continued pursuit of religion and social truths.

Imam Mohammed's astute leadership, profound social commentary on major issues, piercing scriptural insight into the Torah, Bible and Qur'an, and his unique ability to apply scriptural interpretation to social issues have brought him numerous awards and high honors. He is a man of vision who has performed many historical 'firsts'.

In 1992, he delivered the first invocation in the U.S. senate to be given by a Muslim. In 1993 he gave an Islamic prayer at President William Jefferson Clinton's first inaugural interfaith prayer service, and again in 1997 at President Clinton's second inaugural interfaith prayer service. His strong interest in interfaith dialogue led him to address the Muslim-Jewish conference on March 6, 1995, with leaders of Islam and reform Judaism in Glencoe, IL. In October of 1996, Imam Mohammed met Pope John Paul, II, at the Vatican, at the invitation of Archbishop William Cardinal Keeler and the Focolare Movement. He met with the Pope again, on October 28, 1999, on the "Eve of the New Millennium" in St. Peter's basilica with many other world-religious leaders.

In 1997, the Focolare Movement presented him with the "Luminosa Award", for promoting interfaith dialogue, peace, and understanding in the U.S.

In 1999, Imam Mohammed served on the advisory panel for Religious Freedom Abroad, formed by Secretary of State

Madeline Albright. He assisted in promoting religious freedom in the United States and abroad.

In April, 2005, Imam Mohammed participated in a program that featured, "a conversation with Imam W. Deen Mohammed and Cardinal George of the Catholic Archdiocese."

There are many more accolades, achievements and accomplishments made by Imam W. Deen Mohammed. His honorary Doctorates, Mayoral, and Gubernatorial Proclamations give testament to his recognized voice, and the benefit of his leadership to Muslims and non-Muslims alike. He was appointed to the World Supreme Council of Mosques because of the value of his work and leadership in America.

Today, the dignity and world recognition Imam Mohammed has generated is seen all across the world.

Purchase Copies Of This Publication:

WDM Publications
PO Box 1944, Calumet City, IL 60409

Phone: 708-862-7733
Email: wdmpublications@sbcglobal.net

www.WDMPublications.com

For More On Imam W. Deen Mohammed

The Ministry of Imam W. Deen Mohammed
PO Box 1061, Calumet City, IL 60409

Phone: 708-679-1587
Email: wdmministry@sbcglobal.net

www.TheMosqueCares.com